Wounded

(Based on a True Story)

© 2016 By Adrian Miguel Nunez (USMC)

TABLE OF CONTENTS

INTRODUCTION

Chapter 1: Born in East L.A.

Chapter 2: Childhood and Running Wild

Chapter 3: Foster Families, Escape, and Group Homes

Chapter 4: YA, Puberty and New Families

Chapter 5: The Medellins'

Chapter 6: Greetings from Uncle Sam

Chapter 7: Hello Vietnam

Chapter 8: Search and Destroy

Chapter 9: On the Road to 180

Chapter 10: W.I.A. (2/13/69)

Chapter 11: Japan

Chapter 12: Back to the World

Chapter 13: Back to Bragg

Chapter 14: More Blood Spilled

Chapter 15: Mike

Chapter 16: Wedding Bells and a Baby

Chapter 17: Hodgkin's Disease, You S.O.B.

Chapter 18: Life's Blessings and Horrors

Chapter 19: Balancing Act

TABLE OF CONTENTS

Chapter 20: Don't Call Me Sir!!!! I Work for a Living

Chapter 21: My Religious War

Chapter 22: Our War Back Home

Chapter 23: Rollin' Solo in a Constant Blur

Chapter 24: Grazin' in the Grass till the Snow Came

Chapter 25: Tumbleweeds and Hayseeds

Chapter 26: Victory Dance and Las Vegas Runs

Chapter 27: Three Straight Knockdowns

Chapter 28: High Stakes Gambling

Chapter 29: My Ultimate Comeback on the Road to Glory

Chapter 30: A Trail of Tears Down Lonely Street

Chapter 31: Bouncing Back: One Day at a Time

"The pain that you've been feeling, can't compare to the joy that's coming."

-ROMANS 8:18-

INTRODUCTION

I'd always been the underdog. All six of us Nunez children were. There was always that stereotype if you were Mexican and from the hood' you'd become a criminal. Totally false. The story I am about to tell you is 1000% uncut and uncensored. I will try to convey to you my honest feelings and words at each particular time or event. I just wanted to tell you the story of our family. The struggles are real, the fights are real, and the wars we fought were real.

Reading this you'll hear me speaking vulgar language. For that I apologize. These were my honest thoughts and actual events that shook my soul. Whether it was good or bad, it didn't matter. We were used to having the odds stacked against us. The only way in life you can beat those odds is to succeed. You can't argue success. It's impossible. If someone tells you different, walk away. They're selling you horse apples.

I'm sure there are hundreds and hundreds of stories like ours. We grew up raw, grew up tough, and made our bones the hard way. Society wants most to conform to their brainwashing ways. We are the exact opposite. We were UNBREAKABLE. We had an abundance of pride and never quit. Our oldest sister Mary was a whiz at this. She's a poster child for that saying "making a dollar out of 15 cents." Hustling has been built in our blood. Whether we were doing it legal or illegal, we were doing it. Straight facts.

Most people who never lived in the streets have misconceptions of the world. When most hear about "foster kids" they think of garbage. The dregs of the juvenile world. That too is false. Like us, many suffered by the poverty pawned on us. Some parents had no choice and some did. I'm not here to trash my parents or any others. I'm just being real about my story out of my eyes. I've had to relive good moments and some really DARK ones. Reading this kept me up some nights.

My ultimate goal is to praise the Lord and bring hope to others. I know how it is to be dirt poor. Hungry for food so bad that I'd eat mayonnaise straight out of the jar. Wish sandwiches by the dozen. They were meager times. The world has changed for the worse I believe. Back then people were struggling to make ends meet. Times were brutal.

I apologize beforehand for making derogatory marks against certain races. When I was fighting in the Vietnam War, those were my true feelings. After the war and once I healed, I was normal. I've never been a prejudice individual nor am I today. War is hell though. I was young and serving my country. If you're told to kill, you KILL. NO EXCEPTIONS. Killing these soldiers on the other side haunted me for a long time. My only source of help was the Bible and going to church. It has brought me peace as I've confronted my demons head on. I'm not going to preach to you in this story about scriptures and writings. You must seek redemption from within. Nobody can make this happen but YOU. The word is out there for everyone and in arm's reach. All you have to do is grab it and hold on tight. The roads we crisscross in life are never smooth. If there weren't bumps in the road, we'd never learn how to move forward. The

Lord walks beside each and every one of us. We sometimes destroy ourselves; he doesn't.

I'll take you to depths of my life after Nam and the headaches we had to deal with here in the States. The way I was thinking as a young husband, a young father, and a lost, battle-worn soldier. My fight with the VA also. It still leaves a bad taste in my mouth to this day. Although the VA has become better, there's still much more to establish for our veterans returning home. Much more.

I'm also going to take you inside my five failed marriages. It is nothing to be proud of yet nothing to hide. I had issues that came home with me from the war. I had trouble adjusting just like other vets did. We had seen hell from our eyes. Things that humans should never witness. They ruined relationships and friendships at times. It's just the truth I'm telling you.

My rampant drug use was as real as it can get. I didn't hold an episode back. Some might think I'm arrogant or a hypocrite after you read this. That's your opinion. I tried to recollect each memory as best as I could. Just speaking from the heart. Speaking the facts. The facts in this story might be powerful for some eyes. Please remember to read this with an open mind. You won't be reading "The little engine that could."

I've compacted all my failures on one side. All my winners on the other side. Rise and fall after rise and fall. My last move I executed was I rose once again. You cannot keep us down nor count us out. We're defiant. It's in our blood. There's a flood of heartbreak and blood tears. Yet there's also the happiest, blessed moments I relish in to this day. After all is said and done, I have more wins than losses. I can honestly say my ambition and the will to live kept me hungry. It kept me driven.

Throughout my life I have given thanks to the Lord. I want to give thanks to all the people who kept encouraging me to stay in church no matter how difficult life became. My church members from the Seventh Day Adventist Church in Sylmar back in the 70's and 80's. Also to my fellow church members today from the Community Adventist Fellowship. I'll never forget your kind hearts and the love you all so dearly have shown me.

I say this to you the reader: If hope is what you're looking for, read this story front to back. If you have never witnessed or heard of a miracle described in detail, stand by. In this story your eyes will be illuminated to many of life's setbacks and blessings. You will understand and see how life really is for someone who lacks the basic resources. Again this isn't no bakery. There will be no sugarcoating!!! That I promise. Just a story the way I remember it. Judge me if you want. I'm not worried. Only God can judge me. Anything else is irrelevant. Ready to ride a wild roller coaster of life? If so, buckle your seatbelt and lace up the gloves. LET'S GET READY TO RUMBLE!!!!!!!!!!!!!!!!!!!!!!!!!!

My name is Santiago Jim Nunez. This is my story.

9

Chapter 1: Born in East L.A.

My journey into the world began on February 12th, 1949. I (Santiago Jim Nunez) was born at LAC/USC Medical Center aka General Hospital. Most people I know were born here back in the days as hospitals weren't a dime a dozen as they are now. The buildings itself look like off white colored stacks of legos. This is the same hospital featured at the beginning of the soap opera named "General Hospital. "Yes, the one that starred Fiona Hughes and Tristan Rogers. That's my birthplace.

I was born to Manuel Nunez and Bertha Valenzuela. My parents were both Mexican-American. My mother was born in El Paso, Texas as was my father I'm told. I can't tell you much about my father since I never knew him. Whatever I knew of him was told to me by my mother. A fart in the mind so to speak. As I said before, I don't recall any times he was in our lives. I can't say whether I was happy or sad since it's been so long. Later in life my sister Mary had discovered he had been treated in a psych ward sometime in his life. We all have our demons I guess. I heard he passed away in 2004 in San Jose, CA.

My mother Bertha is a whole different story. She was born in Texas and had six sisters. These women were raised rough and raw. Let me just say that they would be the first to participate in a barroom brawl. Things like that didn't scare them, didn't faze them. My mother was known for her brash temper. Also her "live like I'm dying attitude." She would sit around talking for hours on end with her sisters. We'd wake up and they would be awake before us. Hard times they were. She just knew how to survive and make it. It was embedded in her skin.

She always had a loving heart and even though I often doubted it, I knew she loved us all.

East Los Angeles itself was the hub of all other adjoining cities. It was rich in many aspects except for money. You can get the best handmade tortillas, Mexican food, and great handmade clothing here. Most of the streets even today are still lined with peddlers of all sorts. From people selling elotes and raspados to the criminal element selling drugs. Most people here in East L.A. Boyle Heights area are prideful and have deep roots going back four or five generations. Street gangs were always here before my birth and still are today.

My parents had a house on Boulder Street. Years later, Nacho and some neighborhood kids formed a football team named The Boulder Rockers. They were more than a football team. According to Nacho, much closer to a brotherhood. Anyways for most of us who grew up here, the great places to eat here are Al n Bea's, El Tepeyac , and Ciro's to name a few. We used to go to Zody's and Sears to go shopping for the latest when money was available. Most times I can remember we were on welfare.

The other great thing about living in East L.A was the history. Olvera Street which is located in downtown LA, displays many historical works of art featuring Mexican heritage. Also it features many authentic Mexican cookeries, bars, and museums. If you want to travel by train North or South, you can catch the Amtrak at Union Station. People who break the law end up at LA County Jail located on Bauchet Street. I have been there once on a traffic warrant. It was a complete mess. I don't care to visit that hellhole anytime again nor have I since then.

11

Let me introduce you to my siblings. There's a total of six Nunez children. It all began with my sister Mary. She was always lanky and light but heavy fisted. Mary was always strong willed and didn't take shit from nobody even though her size was so small. We all were small but also were lionhearted. Mary used to hustle as a kid in every way possible. Anything to help my mother out with bills, etc. She was the one Mom went to when she needed something from Jons market. Her nickname is "Wela. Or "NAILS" for her toughness.

My brother Nacho was the second eldest and the oldest of the males. He was always into something and street savvy since a young age. He was the one that coordinated all of our little skirmishes with other kids. He'd fight with other kids just to show them that he was small yet way tougher than the average. He wasn't somebody you would call an altar boy but he was the one we all looked up to. He was "Kidd."

My brother Cirilo was born next. We called him "Fritz the Cat." Or just "Cat."

After me came my brother Mike. Mike was the ultimate loner who liked to go off on his own. He felt more comfortable being away and loved that freedom. He would be with us and play with us. He would venture on his own more often. He was the closest brother I ever had. He was an avid reader who loved animals and anything that gave him a rush. He traveled the States doing pro-bull riding as a teenager. We called him "the Nugget." I think we all had that within us. I guess it was just part of life for us.

My baby sister Juanita was the last to be born. She was loveable and much more settle than the rest of us. But she was willing to mix it up with us as we were always causing ruckus. She would always be next to me all the time. You know how it is, some siblings latch on more closely than others. She was also a bit of a follower. I would later learn in the years to come how close Juanita and I would experience. She was definitely a humanitarian since I can remember. A venue she still participates in around the world today.

We all called each other "Kidd." They nicknamed me "the FROG." Yes, I have big eyeballs. My mother Bertha would have an additional seven children from different fathers. But THIS is a Nunez story for the most part. It's where it all started.

Chapter 2: Childhood n Runnin' Wild

Growing up came quick to us kids. I tell you, when you're young it doesn't feel like time flies. To us, it just seems like all of us in the neighborhood were in the same boat. As kids, we would all be playing in the streets together. Usually the women drank beer and/or cooked dinner. The backyards were for the dads who were still there. Ours was gone by 1953 and it was just our Mom raising us. A lot of nights while Mom went out for the evening, it was our older sister Mary and older brother Nacho who ran the house. Most often they were the ones taking care of us, feeding us, and making sure we were safe. They would also be the one to hand us an ass-whooping if we screwed up. We'd all stick together.

While most families had enough it seems like we were always short on everything. One thing that was common was the shortage of food in the house. Although we were on welfare, having six mouths to feed for Mom proved harsh. Often we would all go to sleep starving or sippin' broth since we were so poor. I hated having nothing but it just was the way it was. The idea of living like this didn't sit well with me and I vowed to make things better for us all. Little did I know how ignorant thinking that was at that age. I could barely wipe my own ass for Pete's sake.

One day we were all loaded up into a police car. We all were crying as we were loaded up. We didn't even know where we were going. I'd never live with my mother again. We were dropped off at a hellhole for kids named McLaren Hall. It was a home for kids that were orphans, foster kids, or unwanted. In our case, our mother could not properly care for us anymore and we knew it. She promised to come back for us once she got settled. I knew that was nothing but pipedreams. I couldn't see her stopping her partying ways nor did I look down on her. It hurt a lot knowing she didn't want to stop her ways so she could be with her kids. But you never know what she was feeling or going through. McLaren was a toilet bowl for youths who were not wanted or the "throwaways" as lots of staff members constantly called us. Either way it made me angry when I heard this. It hurt more knowing some of it was the truth.

Sundays at McLaren were a bitch. This was visiting days for those lucky enough to have their biological parents visit them. They'd bring their kids outside food and candy. Others like us didn't get shit and were treated like we were in custody. It sucked feeling that way day in day out. I knew one thing and that was that this: we weren't going to spend years here like some of these kids had. Some kids here had spent over three years or more here. If your parents didn't come pick you up, eventually you could end up in foster homes. That was a whole other beast.

We'd heard horror stories from other seasoned youths at McLaren Hall about foster homes. Some people got foster kids to use them as their slaves, for the state money they were paid, or even worse; to have a little "fun" with the kids. A lot of youths here had a story about being molested or beaten which scared the shit out of all of us. So the idea of going to a foster home someday didn't set well with me at all.

The day came where we were informed that we would soon be placed into foster care permanently. The reality set in that our mother wasn't coming back for us and we would be cast off to some weirdos who for whatever reasons wanted foster kids. I already had a wall up and ready to create havoc if I was picked up by complete strangers. This is the time where I knew it would become true. I was really praying for a nice, loving family like the ones on TV. I always enjoyed watching Lassie and how loving parents they were to Timmy. Shit I was betting on that even though I knew it'd be a 99 to 1 longshot. As the days passed nothing was said. Maybe we'd miss the cut and not be selected. As bad and poor as it was at mother's, that's where we all wanted to go back to. But that just wasn't going to happen. We just wanted to be with our mother. No matter what.

As the weeks passed by it became clear we'd be staying at McLaren Hall a lot longer. There was something else that had us shitting bricks. More and more often, families would be brought in to come meet us. Not just us but different kids there. When it became evident that some of these parents were paying their way to get in and select their own foster kids, we knew we were doomed. Some prospective parents that came into the hall displayed predatory traits. They looked at little girls and boys different. The same way a bodybuilder looks over a piece of steak in the Meat Department.

One day our case worker Mr. Schwartz as we'd coined him comes in our dorm with a smile. He has this beautifulness about him that made me us feel warm. He really cared about us in McLaren. He was one of the few staff there that made a difference. Anyways, he called us six Nunez kids to the table.

His smile gave us a glimmer of hope. It quickly was shattered by the next words he spoke. "I've got great news. You all have been selected to foster homes. You will be paired up in twos and sent to different homes." Different homes my ass!!!!!! We asked why. He said no family could take six kids into one home. It was state rules. We were hit hard with the thought of being separated.

I can already see Mary and Nacho huddling together plotting their escape. There was no way those two were going anywhere. They'd rather go to juvenile hall than a new home with foster parents trying to tell them what to do. I was with that program too but I had been paired up with my baby sister Juanita. I knew I would not abandon her so wherever she went, I was going too. My world as I knew it was going to be over. My new label: FOSTER KID, didn't set well with me. Hell if I felt out of place at McLaren, how the hell was I going to fit in some "Leave It to Beaver" family setting. I told Mr. Schwartz I didn't want to be apart from the others. His hands were tied though. I think it hurt him to see this. I went back to the dayroom to watch TV with the rest of my siblings still at the table. I figured I could get lost in TV and fantasyland thinking I wouldn't be going anywhere but back to our mother's house on Boulder Street.

We're called back to the table by Mr. Schwartz. He told us that he did his best he could to keep us together. He just couldn't produce this time. He was distraught about this. I could tell it was heartfelt. I think back now of how many cases like ours he had to witness. He fought tooth and nail for us kids. He really looked at all of us like we were somebody. He probably took all that hurt home every night. It was like observing homicides left and right. That man will always have my utmost respect. He was a wonderful individual. He wanted the best for all the kids in McLaren Hall.

Chapter 3: Foster Families, Escape, and Group Homes

As promised, within the week, we were all separated and sent away. I can remember Mary and Nacho snickering as they were led out with their new foster parents. We all did. Nobody wanted to leave each other nor Mr. Schwartz's protection. What happened if we ended up in crappy homes where we were just slaves. What if we went to a pervert's house looking to abuse children? We were all bracing for the unexpected.

With that said the four of us were left at McLaren knowing our days were numbered here. We knew we wouldn't going back to Mom's house. The very next day Cirilo, Mike, and my brother Ruben left. Their new foster family were the Ballesteros. They seemed like genuine people to us yet we didn't care. We didn't want to be uprooted period. Yet we didn't have a choice in it. All that was left now was Juanita and I. Anticipation ate the both of us up as each hour passed. We knew we were next.

I told Juanita wherever we went I'd take care of her. I grew up even more once I knew I'd be her father figure/protector. I wasn't going to let some dirt bag hit on my baby sister or touch her in any way inappropriately. I knew that the course of our lives were headed for a head on collision with reality.

After three days we were finally told to pack up our belongings. Our new foster family was here to pick us up. They were the Rodriguez family. The funny part was it was only one woman. Tina Rodriguez. She was a beautiful, Mexican woman who was in her 50's. She had two kids of her own (Jason n Jane). They were very loving just like her. She was very nice to us from the gate. Once we were in her car, she turned off the radio. They wanted to hear all about Juanita and I. She took us to eat lunch before we saw our new home. What a loving woman. Thinking back, I miss her a lot. She treated us with an abundance of love. Mr. Schwartz did us good.

Another great thing that we both found out. Ruben, Cirilo, and Mike were ALSO living in San Fernando not too far from where we were at. The Ballesteros' only lived about three miles away from us. Our case worker wouldn't give out their phone numbers but we found a way around that. We found out where they were going to school and linked up with them two months later. From that point on we vowed to sneak away and meet up as much as we could. I felt we were still a family holding on. It made me smile knowing we all didn't forget our promise we made at McLaren Hall. I was only hoping things were going okay for Mary and Nacho. I had a feeling it wasn't though.

By this time, we had been in a structured setting for three years now. We still hadn't given up on the hope to go back to Mom's but we knew how to manipulate the game. Our foster parents usually made us go to church every Sunday. We came up with this idea that we were going to start attending another denominational religion and they respected that. The only problem was our church on Sundays was the local bowling alley on San Fernando Road. We'd see other kids dressed in nice church clothes such as us and figured out they were up to the same shit we were. We'd hang out with our siblings, exchange stories, smoke cigarettes, etc. We'd laugh about the schemes we were pulling and talk about getting a hold of Mary and Nacho. That was proving to be hard. Later on we found out why.

Mary and Nacho hadn't been at their foster home for more than two weeks. After that, they'd slip out of a window never to return. Turns out while four of us were blessed in good homes, they'd hit one of those evil homes. You know, the ones I've mentioned earlier. We found out later why they ran away. It was horrible to hear their stories.

Mary was being sexually abused by her foster father from the start. Nacho had been getting royal ass-whoopings every single day. They'd seen enough. They were trying to make it home to our mother's house in East L.A. It was a 30-mile trek. After this, they were tagged as "runaways." This wasn't good since you usually ended up in CJH (Central Juvenile Hall) near General Hospital if you were caught. Then they sent you to group homes or other places to house runaways. Nacho called this "bus therapy."

Mary was placed in a convent home run by nuns for about one year. While she excelled in her grades, her mind was already tainted. She'd been through hell and so had Nacho. All for nothing. It wasn't their faults nor any of ours. We just wanted to be with our mother. Things never panned out though as you would think. Mary would soon find this to be true.

Since Mary wasn't in a lockup environment, she walked out one day without notice. She wanted so bad to be reunited with our mother. Soon after this, the police caught up with her. She was granted her wish two months later. The presiding judge granted her application to stay with mom. She was given the golden egg. So she thought at least.

Mary soon found herself being a mother full-time. Let me explain. Over the years my mother had seven other siblings from different fathers. Mary would soon be the babysitter full time. The one to do all the chores. The one to clean up after the youngsters. She was wiped out and never had time to think. Ultimately though, her wish was granted. She became a hustler and would go to the park selling food for money. She'd cook shrimp, tacos, anything she had, to make money. All of her money went to mom. Mary made sure the kids were fed before giving mom her loot. Throughout it all, she was an innocent person stripped of her innocence. Stripped of her chance to be normal. As I look back, hell that's ALL we wanted. Just to be home and live a normal life.

Nacho had been finally caught. He was an avid pot smoker. He went back to an area not far from Mom's neighborhood on 1st Street. He got popped scoring an ounce of pot. When they ran him for warrants, he appeared on the "pop sheet" as WANTED for being a runaway.

Nacho was sent to a group home for troubled youths who were (HRO's) high risk offenders. Upon his arrival, he was knocking out all the bigger older wards. He took control over the whole place. Soon after he was extorting wards for money, drugs, and store. He also made protection money from weaker wards who couldn't fight. Nacho had stacked enough money while busted. After a year, he felt the place had no more to offer him. He climbed a razor wire fence one night after count and wasn't seen for another six months. Time after time this went on for years with Nacho. He'd get locked up, escape, and recaptured. He was stripped of his innocence also. We all were. We were good kids for the most part.

Once again is luck ran out and he was locked up. The judge sent him to a different group home and told him if he blew this opportunity, his next stop would be CYA. That's the California Youth Authority for you squares. It's a youth prison for wards up to 25 years old. Some ex-wards called it "Gladiator School" and it was often referred to as the Last Stop. The judge thought he'd scare Nacho into straightening up. The thing he failed to realize was Nacho didn't fear shit!!!! As he was led out of the courtroom, he blew the judge a kiss. Being locked up came with the territory in his eyes. He didn't give a shit.

One day we were thrown into a whirlwind. We were told by Tina herself that she had to let us go. She had become seriously ill with a rare disease. Her biological kids would have to go with her sister. We had no options. She couldn't care for us. Our world came crumbling down like a Jenga puzzle. We were screwed. Our hearts broke. It wouldn't be the last time.

I still can see the day we were leaving the Rodriguez house. Our case worker showed up and told us we'd have five minutes to get our stuff and say goodbye. We said goodbye to our foster siblings and Tina. As we were getting into our case worker's car, we cried and waved goodbye to Tina and the kids. Off to our new home we went. We were told our new home would be in San Fernando. Still close to brothers living with the Ballesteros'. I must say, we were devastated to be leaving Tina's home. She was a heartwarming woman. She treated us very good. I believe it broke her down more than it does it to leave. She had no choice though. Her time on Earth would be ending in the coming years. Nobody can stop death.

Chapter 4: YA, Puberty, and New Families

We arrived at second foster home in summer of 1961. It was the Rivas family. Mike and Mary Rivas had two daughters (Monique n Jessica) and one son (Mike Jr). Another foster family who were loving and more respectable towards us. Monique and Jessica took to Juanita immediately and introduced her to all their friends as their "sister." Not foster sister but "sister." Mike Jr did the exact same with me. It made us feel like someone really wanted to share their home with us and actually have us be a part of their family. I know the Rodriguez family loved us just as much. It was kind of the same thing here too.

The Rivas family lived on La Rue Street which was one block away from San Fernando High School. I would attend that school in the future. Anyways the Rivas house was a beautifully painted aqua colored and had a nice backyard. Mary had an impeccable garden that spit out nice size tomatoes, squash, onions, corn, etc. She also had fruitful orange and apple trees which we enjoyed daily. One thing that I can remember about the Rivas house was the immaculately placed bowl of fruit on the dinner table. Every piece came from her garden and trees. That was Mary's pride and joy besides her family. Every person who ever walked into the house would go straight to the dinner table and grab a piece of fruit. They knew the bowl was always filled. It was very welcoming.

As the school year approached we begin to get prepared for another new school and new friends. It wasn't hard to meet new friends for me or my baby sister. Our foster siblings could see that and we all would be attending the same school.

Around twelve years old something peculiar started happening that never did: I started liking girls in a BIG way. I was caught kissing girls behind the school buildings and around the playground. Hell I'd get boners if the wind blew and was masturbating at a record pace. My mindset at the time was that I must be the sickest boy on earth. Little did I know this was all standard operating procedure of a growing boy. At that time though I felt like I was a Martian on planet earth.

One other odd thing started to occur. I could see Monique starting to take way too much interest in me. She just spent much more time around me and often situated us where we were alone. When Juanita would go to bed and fall asleep she started waking me up at night. Usually to "talk" in her room. She had her own room as did the others. I chose to share a room with Juanita to make sure she was always protected. The Rivas house was warm and comfortable. Soon I was going to her room every damn night. This was getting weird though.

One night I go to Monique's room and she tells me we are going to watch the Ed Sullivan show. The whole house was asleep and she always had her TV loud. I believed she was losing her hearing in her left ear but she'd never admit it. Anyways I go to her room and Monique is in bed under the covers which wasn't strange since it was raining that night. She tells me to get in bed naked or she'll tell her parents I was trying to force myself on her. FAAAAAAWK!!!! Now I'm up shit creek. Who the hell are they going to believe? Their daughter or a foster kid with an attitude. It was a no-brainer. I was screwed and she knew it. Mind you, I never looked at Monique or Jessica in a sexual way ever. I liked being in the Rivas house and didn't want to leave there. Especially for getting caught boinking one of their daughters. Hell I was still a virgin at 12 years old. I didn't know didley squat about sex. She sure seemed like she did. I plead with her but to no avail. I was checkmated across the board. She had me under the guillotine.

The next thing I remember I was plunging into Monique. That was the night I lost my virginity to Monique. I never asked her if I was her first but I highly doubt it. Maybe she was. Who cares. All I know is that feeling was the best. It felt 200x's better than jerking off I'll tell you that. Nobody told me that I needed to pull out before I came. Well I didn't and exploded inside her. I felt like I was almost pissing in her but way different. As soon as it was over I got my pajamas on and left the room. So much for Ed Sullivan that night, lol.

Juanita n I met Mike and Ruben a few weeks later at Carrillo's for breakfast. That place is still standing as of today. Anyhow, Juanita went to the restroom and I proceeded to tell my bros about my sexual encounter. They countered with their own stories a year ago. They had beat me to it. Those little bastards stole my thunder!!!!! After that I realized we were on destructive paths. Our lives were heading into adulthood at 200mph with no brakes. I guess that's how we've been living our lives since we were kids.

Nacho had pissed away his last chance after he broke out of his second group home. The judge had enough of him and wasn't going to see him in his courtroom again for a long time!!!! He read his sentence to Nacho: "Ignacio Nunez, I hereby sentence you to thirty-six months in the California Youth Authority. I'm sick of dealing with you. Send me a postcard from Disneyland."

Typical Nacho smirked and said," tell your wife I said hello."
Mary came and told us they'd sent "Kidd" to YA. Not only did
they send him to YA but he got 3 years. They were sending him
to the Preston School for Boys. It was in a town called Ione up
North. It would be a while before we would see Kidd on the
streets. His luck had once again run out. To Nacho, it would be
just another place to take over. He still dreamt of being the next
Middleweight Champion of the world. He was a two time
Golden Gloves champion. He'd have a lot of time massacring
sparring partners in YA. An unlimited supply of dumbasses in
there.

Now you might wonder why I mentioned my brother as Kidd.
Well, Nacho was our hero. He would always call us Kidd because
even though we grew a bit older we still fucked around like
animals. We loved it and the name has stuck to this day. Even
my kids, nephews, and nieces still use it. It's our family motto,
and it lives even today.

About three months later I got a letter from Nacho. He said
Preston was a joke and he had "the keys" on his dorm/yard. As
I said Nacho was a mere 5'6, 165lbs of solid brick, and had never
lost a fight. In three months he had destroyed all politics and BS
that the previous fools had held. The other wards enjoyed
Nacho's leadership and charisma, even getting recommendation
letters from YA staff. Those guards were shitheads and STILL he
earned their respect. He wouldn't see daylight till three years
later when he maxed out. By that time the year was 1964 and I
was 15 years old. I'd been smashing every girl in sight and had
built quite a reputation for myself. I kept myself in shape and
even lifted weights. I was a good street fighter too. I was quick
with my hands.

High school had just started and this was absolute HEAVEN to me!!!!! Besides Monique always begging me to pound her one more time, my life was that of a rock star. I was not only excelling in high school grades but I had graduated to a Master's Degree in women. Every corner I turned some girl wanted my attention. I had it down pat, I really did. Back then going to high school was like going to prom every day. The girls were so hot that it wasn't even funny. Natural beauty only. None of this botox and fake bosoms like you can buy now.

I loved the fact that going to school was like going to a day club. I loved going to parties, meeting new girls, and playing music. I have always loved music and loved singing. I finally started to play the saxophone and joined a band called "The Excessions." I was killer on the sax and every time I played that instrument I felt like Elvis Presley onstage at the Las Vegas International. That's the power of music and anyone who has played an instrument can relate. During breaks I'd go smoke a cigarette or share a dubey with the other band members. I must say I liked smoking grass. It kept me relaxed and I enjoyed the high. If I wasn't doing that I was making out with a girl in her car. Then the band would be calling me back inside.

Around this time my band started doing gigs at school and garage parties making a little extra money. It was paradise being paid to do something you love. I loved playing so much I even joined my church choir to sing. It just made me feel alive and my heart was always beating to a drum.

I told Mr. Rivas I was also going to look for a part time job. He said it was a great idea. I needed more money to invest in my band and wardrobe. I loved dressing sharp and would always get multiple compliments. I would never go out looking like crap. Hair had to be done, shoes needed to be shined, and clothes immaculately pressed. That look sets you a cut about the rest and you stand out. It only added to my persona.

A month before Thanksgiving, Juanita and I were summoned to the Mike and Mary's room. Mike instructed me to close the door behind me. Mary didn't even look at us. I knew what this meant. Our time was up at the Rivas house. He didn't even have to say a word. They both expressed to us how much they loved us and they wish they could adopt us. But the courts took forever and it wasn't going to be in time. Back then you usually got moved every two or three years. I didn't want to leave but then again a change would be good. Too much comfort meant you sometimes got slow. After all we were just visitors no matter how you looked at it. We still belonged to the courts. I wondered how our next foster home would be like. The thing was, Juanita and I had made it through hell this far. There was no quitting or turning back. We'd been fighting too long to submit now.

Chapter 5: The Medellins'

We said our goodbyes to the Rivas family and jumped into our case worker's car. I must say we were excited a bit and wondered where we'd be going now. As it turns out, we were headed to Pacoima near the Whitman Airport. That's the little airport that Cessna planes took off from. It had close to seven hangars and multiple lines of planes. Also right near the train tracks where roaring rail cars screamed through town after town carrying goods statewide. I loved the scenery and we took it all in. As we made a right onto Pierce Street, our case worker told us we were almost there. One left onto Telfair Avenue and there it was. Our new home. A big home too with a sprawling backyard that extended all the way to the next street. I could see I was going to love it here. Little did I know how much this place would change us.

We got our bags off and our case worker introduced us to our new foster family named The Medellin family. Robert and Maria were the parents. They had four kids of their own: Robert II (Bobby), Hanky, Patricia, and Evelyn. They seemed way up on respect and love. I will NEVER forget the way Maria hugged us and told us that she loved us. The funny thing is that she was 100% genuine and I felt it. To be honest, I hadn't even felt that kind of love from my own mother. What a feeling of being wanted and loved. Robert was a man of heart, balls, and stone all wrapped in one. He ruled the house with an iron fist and wasn't so emotional. He wasn't big on compliments either. One thing he perfected was supporting his family and chasing his dreams. He made his dreams become realities. He came from an abusive home. His father was a raging alcoholic who handed him and his siblings their asses on a constant basis. He built his trucking business "MEDELLIN TRUCKING" from nothing. A high school dropout who failed to go in the U.S. Navy during WWII, he married Maria when they were just 15 to get out of their homes. He promised her the world and a better life. He produced TENFOLD!!!!!!

Also living in the back house was Maria's father Kinteen. This guy was something else. He was over 60 years old and was a character. He'd often tend to the garden during the day. Then at night he'd take the bus to the San Fernando mall. He frequented a few bars in the mall. There he'd get blasted and mess with his many women. Maria always worried about him. He was like a 60-something year old pimp, lol. He wore slacks, nice shoes, nice collared shirt, and ALWAYS rocked a Fedora with a feather. He smoked Lucky Strike non filter cigarettes and lived like he was 16 at times. But we loved him and his ways. Often at the dinner table he'd wait to see if his plate was even than Robert's. If not, Maria had to fix it and make it even. I guess it was a machismo thing. Robert would just smirk towards his direction and shake his head. I respected Robert more for that.

I got along with all my new siblings and we all went to school together with the exception of the boys. They went to Poly High school in Sun Valley. Bobby had just graduated. He told Mom and Dad that he was going to sign up in the US Air Force and going to the Vietnam War. It had just kicked off and the war was gaining minutes on the nightly news. I saw Mom's face when Bobby told her that. Little did she know this wouldn't be their only son going to Vietnam. Poor woman looked devastated. She tried to hide it but I saw right through it. Hell, I'd been raised in a world of devastation. I knew what it looked like and what it smelled like. There was no bullshitting me when it came to pain.

We settled in and got used to the functions at the Medellin house. Very structured and ran like clockwork. Dad used to get up at 310am and start up all five trucks in the yard. Mom would start coffee and his breakfast. She'd have a meal ready for us all by the time we woke up. I loved this. It feels great when you are a part of something so loving, so valuable.

Hanky also went to Poly high school so it was me and the girls walking two miles each way to San Fernando High School. It was a trek but it was a great chance to get to know my sisters. They were very different in their own ways. Patsy was a girl who wore no makeup, loved to hunt bugs, ride horses, and wrestle with her brothers. She had a lot of friends at school. She said she had met me before and thought I was a conceited prick. Nice to meet you too sis.

Evelyn was a whole different ball of wax. She was an avid reader who rarely left the house. She had a smart mouth on her but hey she was still my little sister. She was the baby of the family and treated as such. I know that I used to get a kick out of her and Patsy. Always arguing when she wanted Evelyn to go outside and play. Evelyn refused 9 out of 10 times. One thing I will say is Evelyn could blow through a 300- page book in a matter of 5 hours. I know I didn't qualify. I was too busy chasing tail and playing my sax. That was my career at the time.

Hanky used to hang out with me and we'd go score girls together. We both smoked cigarettes and drank jungle juice behind Dad's shed in the backyard. I could easily go to the back near the cactus plants and smoke a joint. I did of course. One time Kinteen saw me smoking. He asked what the hell I was doing behind the cactus. I told him I didn't want to get caught by Dad. He said he wouldn't say anything and he didn't. His nose must've gone to shits by then. He never caught on that I was smoking grass. I got a kick out of it.

Dad also had some property out in Ensenada, Baja California, Mexico. It was a five-hour drive from Pacoima but it was heaven. Dad used to pack us all in and head down there for a week during the summer. He had converted a trailer camper and built a house attached to it. Right in front of the beach. You could throw a rock from the front door and hit water. Dad had built a massive break wall in case the hurricanes and storms caused major waves. Summer after summer, Dad's house was the only one that didn't suffer any damage. Waking up on the beach in Ensenada was like a dream come true. The ocean smell reminded me of fresh baked Mexican sweet bread. Mom would be cooking breakfast and after an hour wait we'd all be in the ocean for the whole day. Juanita and I would play chicken fights in the water against other kids from the neighboring campground La Jolla. We felt like the luckiest foster kids on earth.

I had a job at a fast food restaurant called Jack in the Box. I had friends pass by and I'd hook them up with tons of free food. Every day I had a new girl's number since I operated the drive thru. Things with the band were excellent. My buddy Rudy and I started ditching school at an alarming rate. I figured I'd covered my end and wrote my own absentee notes. We'd go to L.A. and meet older girls over there. It was lovely. Until one day on the 5 freeway sacked my ass.

Dad traveled every street and highway due to his trucking business. One day Rudy and I had picked up these girls from Simi Valley. We were headed to East L.A. to party over there since I figured we'd be safe. As we passed the Hollywood Way exit, I saw Rudy turn to me like he saw a ghost. "NUNEE, look over there to your left." I peeked to the left and saw Dad looking dead at us. He was driving one of his trucks. He knew Rudy's car and now we locked eyes. He pointed at me with a serious face and I read his lips: "I'll see you later." FUCK ME!!!! What's the chances of running into Dad on the damn freeway? 100 to 1. GEEZZ!!! Rudy asked what we were going to do. I replied "nothing let's go have fun. I'm already busted. I'll face the music tonight."

Dad handed me a verbal ass-chewing from outer space. He told me I'd be a failure if I didn't get my shit straightened. The next day we were headed to San Fernando High School. Dad wanted to see my attendance records for himself. As we got to the school, I saw Evelyn who was a teacher's aide for the office. I went up to her desk and pleaded to her. "Throw all those absentee slips out of my file. Otherwise I'm SCREWED." She agreed to help. We sat in the office and waited. About thirty minutes later, my counselor arrived. He escorted us into a room. He sat with Dad and I with my file in hand. It was STILL an inch thick. DAMNIT Evelyn!!!! I thought she was going to help me. I was going to strangle her when I saw her again. Dad found out about my shenanigans I had been pulling. I confessed. I didn't even try to hide it. Dad had me cornered. I promised to do better and I did. I hated disappointing that man. I later got a hold of Evelyn and asked her why she hung me to dry. She told me she'd thrown out over half my file. DAMN. I was content with that. She tried her best.

There was only one problem: Juanita. She was talking constantly about going back to live with our biological mother. I honestly had forgotten about that years ago and was too content to move back now. I had suffered enough and I knew I wouldn't have this kind of life at our mother's. I told Juanita if she ran away from here I wouldn't be going with her. She'd be on her own. It was a tough but yet easy decision. I had grown close to Mom and Dad like nobody before. I loved having talks with them both. Dad was teaching me mechanics and how to be a man. Mom was always helping me get over things from the past. I had nice foster siblings. Yeah I was sold. I got hooked on their love, their unity, their family. I wasn't leaving no way no how.

Like I figured, Juanita ran away and never came back. I knew she was back at our biological mother's but I had no care to live there. My life was at its peak by now. I had things going for me now like never before. Dad was mentoring me in so many ways that I became addicted to it. I could now change the trucks' tires, break down engine components, check the air brakes, etc. I also was excelling in my band and mastering the sax as each day passed.

Then came a crushing blow. Hanky was going to Vietnam. He enlisted to be a paratrooper in the 101st Airborne Division which was a kick ass outfit. In 1966, he was gone to the Army. I was still a junior in high school but the Vietnam War was taking center stage of every conversation, every television screen. I saw more and more friends enlisting but I was still too young to join. It became a part of my daily thoughts. I prayed for my two brothers in Vietnam now. I could see Mom smoking at the dinner table with Dad. They would stare at each other but wouldn't say it. You could feel their worry, their pain. In my heart I knew I would eventually add to it once I joined. I kept that to myself though.

Chapter 6: Greetings from Uncle Sam

I had decided that I'm going to enlist in the United States Army. I am going to be a paratrooper. Maybe I can join up with Hanky and our cousin Amador who was in Vietnam in the US Marines. It was time for me to go. I was ready to get out and serve my country. Mom and Dad were pretty quiet the day I left. I told them I loved them and I'd be back once my two years were done. It was November 1967 and I was gone. I was heading to Fort Ord in Monterrey California for eight weeks of basic training.

"Get off my bus you fuckin' maggots. HURRRRRYY UP!!!!" Those were the first words I can remember the Drill Sergeant screaming as he climbed onto the bus. We all scrambled off and were told to line up in formation. While some people shit in their pants, I actually enjoyed this kind of stuff. It made me feel proud that I was about to enter a new chapter in my life. Once I was finished with the military, I'd move on and open my own business just like Dad had done. Maybe I'd work for Dad or buy his business. I enjoyed the trucking industry. Dad was set for life. I had no idea how much the military would be stuck in my life forever.

The first week was a bunch of boredom. The only thing we seemed to do was get a ton of shots and fill out mountains of paperwork. These drill sergeants constantly were yelling down our necks and talking in this innocuous form of talk. It was pure military jargon. Then we were issued our gear and uniforms. Now it seemed we'd get the ball rolling. We did PT (physical training) every morning at 430am. I personally loved PT and became road guard. Then I became a squad leader and stuck through it the whole eight weeks.

The second week was much better and we were actually learning. We got map training extensively. We drilled our butts off, and learned some navigation. Shooting an azimuth would prove vital in Vietnam since the terrain over there was ridiculously mountainous. Some of the drill sergeants who had been to Vietnam would stress this so much.

The third week was totally for medic training and how to do the basics. We were taught all kinds of ways to plug wounds, shrapnel wounds, etc. This is when it became reality that most of us soon would be doing this real time. Combat medics also went through courses on how to do the basic tourniquets, etc. I was like a sponge soaking up all this information. I knew I'd need it down the road.

The fourth week we'd march more in our OD greens and combat boots. Jungle boots were issued to those heading to Vietnam. We did a variety of humps and were simultaneously ambushed by drill sergeants firing LIVE rounds. The first time I saw "the PIG" I knew I wanted one. The PIG is what they called the "M-60" machine gun. It was gas operated and belt fed. It had a bi-pod and it weighed 24 pounds unloaded. I fell in love right there.

Rifle qualifications came next along with grenade throwing and pistol quals. I loved touching any kind of weapons and the M-14 was a beauty. It was heavy (14 pounds loaded I believe) but accurate as hell. I loved the rifle and it spit out 7.62 rounds. The same rounds the PIG shot out. I qualified expert at everything I touched. I would pay attention to the drill sergeants especially the ones who were Vietnam vets. I could see there was a difference in them than the others. They had this dark, deep look in their eyes. I later would find out that was called "the thousand-yard stare." It was a gaze into yonder, a look that displayed a soldier had seen too much combat, too much death.

Graduating boot camp was a great feeling. I was ready to move on and now headed to the San Francisco airport. My destination was Fort Benning Georgia for three weeks of jump school. After jump school I would get my permanent duty station. That's when they tell you where you'll be stationed for the remainder of your contract.

Fort Benning was very different than Fort Ord. Fort Ord was always foggy and cold for the majority of the time I was there. It was so close to the ocean and you got that chill every morning. Also it was rain constantly in Ord. Benning was like the air was sucked out from a vacuum and you got hot air in return. To top that off, the humidity was abusive. You'd be outside for a minute and your blouse was soaked in sweat. I just hated the humidity. But I was only going to be there for only three weeks so I sucked it up and drove on.

Our instructors called black hats (because they wore black baseball caps with jump wings on the front) and we were told we'd be running everywhere we went. If you were going to the PX you'd be running. If you were going to chow, you were running. If you were going to kill yourself, you'd do it running!!!! Get my point. We'd spend the week building our legs up and practicing PLF's (parachute landing falls). It was pretty exciting hanging on makeshift lines and falling five feet into sandpits. You are supposed to land ankle-knee-quad-hip-shoulder. In that exact order. It never happens that way 100% of the time.

The second week was tower training nothing but. We were hoisted in a tower with an open parachute 250 feet off the ground. Then they dropped you and the black hats would be screaming at you to pull your risers this way that way. Your risers were your steering wheels for your parachute. I had a blast doing this. After the week was over I was ready for week three: JUMP WEEK.

To become airborne qualified, you must complete five jumps including a night jump. When we were getting our parachutes rigged on, you could barely walk. It was so tight on you and it make your groin section bulge to a gigantic size. Once in the air, the pilots dipped and dove knowing we were all cherries. Once we reached our altitude, we were told to hook up and scuffle to the door. I could see the jumpmaster open the door and stick his grape out looking for the DZ (drop zone). Then the starboard side begin moving once the green light went on. I was on the port side and our side started moving. In an instant I was being shitted off the C-130 along with the others. The view was gorgeous and my chute opened perfectly. I landed with no hiccups and yearned to go back up asap. Four more jumps followed and I was officially a US Paratrooper.

The jumpmasters would pin your jump wings on but not put on the backings of them. This exposed the sharp edges. They'd go to you and say "congratulations Airborne" and push the wings into your flesh. It hurt like a motherfucker but you had to stand there and take it. Hence the term "blood wings "were born. Next thing was to get our orders. I couldn't wait to see where I was going next. I finally got my orders and it read: Fort Bragg, North Carolina. Home of the Airborne.

I was in Fort Bragg in three days and excited to see my new home. The air was the same like it was in Georgia but a bit cleaner. There were tall trees all around and forestry setting. Pope Air Force base stood next door which was our loading dock so to speak. I got familiarized with the place pretty fast and the neighboring towns. I was attached to a unit that was a 105mm artillery battery. The arty boys are the ones who loaded the rounds, set coordinates, and one soldier attached with a cord turned. In that instant the cannon blasted out the round and expended the shell casing. I found this to be fun at first but quickly became bored. I needed action, wanted action.

I wanted to go to Vietnam and get the hell out of North Carolina. After 16 months there, I had seen enough. I was sick of this hick town and wanted out. This place was boring!!!! Lumberton, Hay Street, and everything else around Bragg didn't cut it for me. I placed transfer orders to Vietnam over and over. FINALLY, I was granted my wish. I thought to myself, "anything is better than this. How bad could Vietnam be?" Soon I'd be putting my foot in my ass.

Two weeks later I was on a C-130 taking a flight to Fort Lewis, Washington. This was the final stop before leaving to Vietnam. This was it. When I arrived there, I was whisked to the civil affairs office to fill out paperwork. Reality hit me when the life insurance policy sheet was put in front of me. I asked the clerk "Why am I signing this for?" His response was eye opening. "So when your body's splattered in the sky we know who gets a check for your service." DAMN like that? Some compassion I thought. It was the ignorance in me. It hadn't sunk in that I was heading to a meat grinder 10,000 miles away. It was called the Vietnam War.

I didn't give a shit. I said to myself "I'm Jim Nunez. I've lived a hard life and survived." I was proud I was going to Vietnam. I had heard it was hell on earth. I was going to adapt and overcome no matter what it took. All my training, all my teachings I soaked up, I felt prepared. The Army had done its job getting me ready. Now I was ready to kick ass and kill.

Chapter 7: Hello Vietnam

I vividly remember flying out of Fort Lewis on that hot, summer day. I was ready to get the hell out of the US and go fight in Vietnam. In three years plus, the war had become full blown. The Vietnamese had been fighting for over a thousand years and were unrelenting. As poor as they were, they'd been whipping everyone and anyone who came to conquer. They knew the land like the back of their hand. Fighting wasn't shit to them.

The USA had sent "advisers" in Vietnam since the 50's in hopes of communism not spreading. Hence the domino effect was born. It was dually noted that if Vietnam fell to communism, all other neighboring countries would as well. The times of Cold War were intense and threats were traded back and forth. The Soviet Union had been caught just six years ago storing ICBM's (intercontinental ballistic missiles) in Cuba just 90 miles south of Miami, Florida. That's the fancy word for nuclear warheads. Tensions were still high. Come to think of it, I still remember school having "bomb drills" in case we were attacked. It was no joke. We all took it seriously.

After a stop in Hawaii and Japan, I finally landed in Vietnam 36 hours later. DAMN was it hot. Purgatory lol. The Devil's Den I thought!!!!! It was in a city named Bien Hoa which was in Southern Vietnam. I was" SUPPOSED" to be placed on another flight in a few days to go up north. In the meantime, we were free to roam around town in Bien Hoa. The first day a group of us newbies went out. The people of the town flocked to us like flies on a rump roast. They were trying to sell us everything from watches to gum to soda pop. All of course claiming they had the "numbah one" product. The "white mice" (South Vietnam police) would make go them away and they'd catch up with us on the next street. We headed to some bar with unlimited access to everything. Alcohol, whores, drugs, you name it. I smoked some high potent grass I'd never smoked back in the states. They had the best stuff here.

We got smashed day after day. Plus, I was lost in the system and ended up staying in Bien Hoa for three long weeks. While I was there, it was a straight party nonstop. I made some friends with some of the "old-timers" who had time in country. They were awesome friends who showed me the town upside down. I almost forgot this country was at war with us. My three weeks were filled with laughter and amazing times.

 My very first thing I remember was getting off the plane and feeling like I was in a damn sauna. The weather was a boiling pot. It was unbearable. I thought the landscape was so gorgeous as were the pristine rivers that littered the country. Rice paddy and dikes were scattered everywhere. The locals were geniuses and used water buffalos to graze their paddies. I couldn't even imagine a war was going on here. Again the ignorance of mine. We were also told we called the enemy "Charlie, Victor Charles, or Nathaniel Victor." They all coincided with the phonetic alphabet (C=Charlie, VC=Viet Cong, NVA=North Vietnamese Army). A ton of more derogatory ones were commonly used also: "gooks, dinks, slants zipperheads." Get the picture.

We were divided up and sent to units that needed replacements. I was going to the 101st Airborne Division and couldn't be happier. My brother Hanky was on his second tour in Vietnam and I hoped to run into him soon. After a two-hour flight we landed in a city named Phu Bai. I was then bussed to my new home called LZ SALLY. I was part of Bravo Company, the 1/502nd or "Deuce" as they called it. It was in the middle between Camps Evans and Eagle. We were in I Corps as they called it. Operating in the Quang Tri Province less than 60 miles away from the DMZ (demilitarized zone). That line separated North and South Vietnam. Less than 10 klicks to the West was the infamous "A Shau Valley." To the North was the Ruong Ruong Valley. Another NVA beehive. Even the seasoned vets would tell you it was a hellhole there. It was Charlie's basecamp of all basecamps. The VC (Viet Cong) were mainly villagers by day and fighters by night. They lived in the vils (villages) along the land scattered throughout the country. NVA (North Vietnamese Army) were different. Uniformed, highly trained and well equipped, the A Shau Valley was their backyard. This is where they lived. Hell they even had generated power and mail there. Need I say more.

Once at LZ Sally we were issued our gear and our new weapon (M-16A1) rifle. It was 7 pounds loaded and felt like a damn toy. I preferred the M-14 or some other weapon. It shot 5.56 rounds instead of the 7.62 rounds fired by the 14 or 60. I looked at it and said to myself "I gotta get me a stronger weapon than this." We were issued five frag grenades as well as different colored smoke, and Willie Pete's (white phosphorus). Different colors of smoke were to be popped to warn the Huey pilots coming to insert or extract us. If it was a "hot zone" meaning gooks all around us, you'd pop red smoke. If there was no danger at all, we'd pop green smoke. It was an effective method and gave the pilots a heads up. It helped the pilots land perfect in the LZ's (landing zones).

There were five of us that were replacements and shown to our cots in our tents. Most of the vets who had time in hated us and called us FNG's. That stood for Fucking New Guy. They didn't want nothing to do with us but we were part of the team. We just had to earn their respect and not screw up in the field. Our platoon sergeant gave us a rundown of what to expect and what to look out for. Not an hour later after we'd gotten some hot chow, the whole camp erupted and constant yells of "INCOMING" echoed in between blasts. The continuous sounds of "CRUUUUMP, CRUUUUMP "made the ground shake as enemy rockets chewed into the red clay earth. One mortar rocket found its mark. It blew one of our latrines to shits. Literally!!!! I grabbed my rifle and beat feet into a nearby foxhole. After a few minutes the screeching sounds of artillery could be heard hitting our enemy targets outside the wire. Next we heard "fastmovers" (fighter jets) drop their payload of napalm and scorch the jungle in an instant. Like that it was all over. My heart was beating 200 a minute damn near. I was scared to death. This was just my FIRST day. In Vietnam you did one year tours. That was 365 and a wake up. I still had to survive 364 more!!!!!!!

Being "inside the wire" was supposed to be our safety zone. For the most part it was. Inside the wire meant being in basecamp which was surrounded by rolls upon rolls of concertina wire. There were empty beer cans attached to the wire incase Charlie came snooping around. It would alert the OP (observation post). Rocket attacks and Sapper charges were your worst fears.

Two weeks in country at LZ Sally, unbeknownst to me, Mom (Maria) had been writing letters to Congress saying she had already two sons in Vietnam and I was the third. She didn't want all her sons there and feared the worst. The military tried their best after WWII not to send siblings overseas for combat fearing the entire family would be killed in action. It still happened but wasn't as common. It sent mad publicity throughout the states after WWII and they didn't want to repeat it again. I had been in Vietnam for two weeks. I was getting familiar with a lot of key elements from the vets who had more time in country. Setting claymores, what smoke to pop, what to look and listen for on watch, etc. I was checking out a map with one of our TL's (Team Leader: usually a Sergeant E-5 or up) when our Company Commander Burney came in our tent. He called out "Private Nunez, where the fuck are you? Where's that FNG Nunez? "I ran to the front of the tent to meet him. "Yes Sir Private Nunez reporting." He shook his head and said "pack up your shit you're going home. I got a letter from the Red Cross saying you don't have to be here since you have two brothers in country already. You lucky motherfucker. I guess Charlie won't be meeting you anytime soon. You got an hour before we take you to Da Nang. You can catch the freedom bird out of here."

"Sir, I'm not leaving with all due respect. It took me fourteen months of hell just to get here. I'm not going back to the world till my tour is over. Now you can tell whoever sent that letter that I'm not going anywhere." Captain Burney came closer and said "you have a ticket outta this hell and you wanna stay? You ignorant FOOL. Some of these guys that are short timers would saw off a limb to get out of here!!! You want to stay? You're the DUMBEST FNG I've ever seen. You must think you're BEAUCOUP DINKY DAU (real crazy in Vietnamese). Well if that's what you want you'll have to sign this declaration saying you decline and chose to stay in Vietnam." That wasn't a problem with me. I knew Mom meant well but nobody was going to dictate what happened to me. I had fought tooth and nail just to get here. Now that I finally made it here, I was supposed to leave? Heck no!!!!! It was my word and I stuck by it. Captain Burney took the paper from me after I signed. As he turned away I heard him utter "dumbass."

Within the hour word had spread what I had turned down. DIWEE (Captain in Vietnamese) made sure of that lol. He told everybody. A lot of soldiers shook their heads in disbelief. Others laughed and mocked me. But they ALL respected me a ton. I had my ticket out of there and chose to stay with them. The attitudes from the seasoned vets changed towards me instantly and they begin to teach me more. One of them Corporal Bell asked "you good firing the 60?" I knew this was going to be good. I smirked and replied "yes I am." "Good, you're going to be one of our 60 gunners. You'll be in 2nd Squad. Congratulations motherfucker. Welcome to the Nam. "

Now my theory was I had a WAY better chance of surviving the Nam' if I had some kickass piece of firepower. So having the M-60 was like hitting the jackpot. It was gas operated and belt fed. I also got an AG (assistant gunner) who's sole job was to hump ammo and feed belts of it to me in case of a firefight. It was also better than walking point. What I DIDN'T know was that Charlie's first objective in a firefight was to knock out the high powered machine guns and grenadiers. That was the category I fell into. Oh shit. I'd soon find out how true this was.

Vietnam was a country full of devastation yet beauty too. Let me point out the terrain itself would put a man in his grave quicker than Charlie could. The weather could easily go from 100 degrees plus to 30 degrees at night. The hills and mountaintops seemed to almost reach the skies. You couldn't see through the thick foliage or bamboo. Tall elephant grass was razor sharp and 10 feet high. Several poisonous and dangerous snakes of the world resided in Vietnam. There were validated stories that a few soldiers had even been killed by a Bengal tiger. Yes a TIGER. I wasn't ready to hear that. Facts are facts though. When it rained in Vietnam it rained in SHEETS!!!! It would come down in such a fierce wall of water. It was like God was watering the whole planet's plants through Vietnam. Monsoon season was the worst.

Charlie's "gifts" that he left for us U.S. troops were a whole different world of terror. The country was full of booby-traps that I'll try to remember them all. Landmines such as "toe poppers and bouncing betties "were the worst. If you stepped on one, you were boned. They also had viper pits which was a hole in the ground covered by makeshift earth. Once a troop fell into the pit he was bitten by venomous vipers, king cobras, and bamboo vipers. Another horrible one was punji pits. There would be bamboo sharpened punji stakes at the bottom of the pit resembling a bed of nails but bigger. The sharp end of the stakes would be dipped in excrement. The infections would kill you if you happened to survive the fall. It would surely maim you at the very least. There were the millions of miles of tunnels throughout the country. Charlie would have firing posts they'd poke out of, let off a magazine from their AK-47 killing troops, then go back in their tunnels. It was like fighting ghosts. It mind-fucked you. These tunnels would have field hospitals, dorms, kitchens, and storage space. All dugs by the Vietnamese by HAND. Incredible. You had to respect these guys. I know I did. They were resilient.

We were told we'd been ordered to go on patrol in the A Shau Valley. Intel had reported a "sapper battalion" (NVA commandos known for satchel and explosive charges) were operating towards the eastern end of the valley. Sappers used to inch their way towards the wire and turn claymore mines around at night. Then they'd set off noise in the area. The American troop on watch would grab the clacker and blow the claymores. Thus shredding American soldiers instead of the enemy.   Time to start earning your pay. They called it "search and destroy" missions. Our objective was to find the enemy and kill them. Gather information and move on. A lot of the terrain in the A Shau had been hit by B-52 "carpet bombings" and left massive craters in the earth. We'd get helo'd in by Huey helicopters (UH-1). Those were our motorized horses. Before we'd get to our LZ (landing zone), we used fake insertions/extractions to fool Charlie where we actually were. LZ watchers/scouts often could be spotted near potential LZ's. They'd be the alarm to the rest of the gooks that US troops were in the vicinity. "Humping the boonies" became our full time job. When you're deep in enemy territory, the man to your left is right is all you have. Somebody screws up it's costly. I prayed to God he'd watch over us.

One day I was learning to set up "daisy chain claymores" from a few vets. Captain Burney came up and told me to report to his field office. Once I arrived there he had another FNG named PFC Mendez there. Captain Burney was puffing on a cigar when he said," you FNG's got shit burning detail. I suggest you take your blouses off while you do this. Go see Sgt. Hayes at the shitters."

56

We meet Sgt. Hayes at the shitters. "You FNG's got this. I left you boys' a present in hole # 1. "He walked off laughing as he launched an empty beer can in a nearby ditch. These were a small latrine (bathroom) built by engineers with six holes. GI's would sit side by side almost to take a shit in these holes. Below it was a half cut 55lb drum with handles on both sides. The lucky bastard on detail would then open up the trap door on the other side. He would pull and drag the drums out. Then mix kerosene in each drum, light it up, and stir it with a metal/wooden stick. It would turn to ashes after a while of cooking this "shit stew." The nastiness and foul odor make me vomit. I hated shit burning detail from that point on. Later I would pay others to do it after. Mendez and I looked like grease monkeys after we were done. Showering didn't help. That shit would be in the wind.

Chapter 8: Search and Destroy

We started out with a gear check. Followed by ammo and water checks. You never knew when we'd hit a river or stream as our water source while out in the field. Maps sometimes would miss certain water sources. Bandoliers of ammo and belt fed ammo were passed around. We'd pack C-Rations, medical bandages, and extra frags. We'd be gone a two week "search and destroy" mission. So we'd have to pack heavy. We'd be dropped off on the outskirts of the eastern end of the A Shau Valley. Our objective was to locate the Sapper battalion supposedly operating around this area. Intel reported they had a basecamp on the east end. We were supposed to kill as many as we could and blow their complex to shits. That is if we even discovered one!!

Sergeant Hayes was our platoon sergeant and one tough son of a bitch. He was a Georgia native who grew up near Stone Mountain. Our "LT" was 1st Lt. Marks. He played some college ball in Arizona before coming to Vietnam. He was smart and knew the terrain very well. Both were on their 2nd tours in Nam.' Both had purple hearts. Both were unbelievable leaders whose charisma and their "no fear" attitudes spread through us all.

We were on our way to the helopad with our 100lb rucksacks on and weapons. Marks and Hayes were joking and laughing as they openly shared a joint. They were talking about DEROS (date estimated to return overseas) coming soon for both. Both were now under 90 days respectively and were talking about their plans once they rotated back to the world. All of a sudden

Sgt. Hayes smiles at me and says "Nunez how many days you got left? 345 I said." Lt Marks and Sgt. Hayes both start laughing their asses off. Sgt. Hayes: "by the time you finish your first tour, LT here will be in Phoenix sitting in his pool. My wife will probably be having our second kid. YOU!!! Well, you'll juuuuuuuust be finishing your tour in the Nam'. IF you make it."

As we were heading to the helopad I saw a glimmer of light. It was my brother Hanky. He'd been in Vietnam for over a year now. 15 months to be exact at the time. He was on his second tour. He was operating in Phu Bai and made his way over to LZ Sally. He'd heard I was in country and wanted to make sure I would be ok. He ended up saving my life. He asked Sgt. Hayes if he could join. He told Hanky "sure."

I hadn't been in a firefight yet. I was carrying the M-60. It was heavy but it was better than walking point. Hanky was schooling me on the terrain and what to look for while we waited. He wanted to make sure I would adjust incase Mr. Charles were to confront us. He was rock solid and he said to stay by his side. In Hanky's words," Little brother if we make contact you better be stuck to my ass like flies on a turd pile. You got it." I nodded yes quickly. He spoke firm but concerned too.

We were inserted in a small clearing. The Hueys' wouldn't land so we had to jump off six feet from the ground. We immediately set up a wagon wheel defensive perimeter. This was to make sure we weren't spotted and to be secured 360 degrees. We "laid dog "for thirty minutes to make sure the coast was clear. We didn't see an LZ watcher or any signs of enemy activity. There were two platoons of us from Bravo and we were hump

60

Northwest. Another vet told us that we'd hit enemy contact along the way. He said he'd bet money on it. I was eager and excited to finally be in the "bush." I hadn't seen an enemy soldier up close or in the battlefield yet. The Viet Cong usually wore black pajamas and conical hats called "Non-La's." The NVA wore uniforms tan colored uniforms with tan colored helmets. They were round like a bush hat. They all wore "Ho Chi Minh" sandals made out of rubber.

The third day we were humping we ran into a small company of gooks. Nathaniel Victor type. (NVA regulars). They opened up on us from three angles. Hence it looked like we'd semi-walked into a V-shaped ambush. Hanky dropped and started firing his rifle. I went to the ground too. I started to get the 60 up near cover when the earth started cracking around me. I FROZE UP!!! It's the worst thing you can do in combat. The next thing I remember is Hanky grabbing the PIG and moving to his right flank. The bravery and courage I witnessed him display was priceless. I was so in awe as I watched my big brother kick ass. He had no fear whatsoever. He loved being in the bush. Hanky wasted seven gooks coming up on the right flank. Every shot was on the money. He tore them to pieces!!!! He adjusted and moved over again to his left flank. He laid down so much suppressing fire the gooks started falling back. He turned and said "JIMMY SNAP OUT OF IT. Lay down some fire on these fucking dinks!!!!" What seemed like an eternity was a mere 10 seconds. But that's enough to get your shit blown sky high. I should've been dead. Hanky had saved my life. I started firing my 45 pistol in rapid session. I nailed two gooks right in the chest. They dropped dead on the spot. Hanky yelled "now that's what I wanna see. Come feed me brother." I bear-crawled over and started feeding him chain linked 7.62 ammo. We managed to escape and evade. We took minimal casualties and wounded.

Sgt. Hayes came up to me and said, "your soul brother needs to be in our unit. That motherfucker's a killer." One thing I'll say about my brother Hanky. That dude belonged in Vietnam. Some of the most courageous acts were shown by him in combat. Hands down. In two tours in Nam, he was never hit. The damage he wreaked on Charlie was hell I could only imagine. One of the best under fire. I wanted to be just like Hanky. I'd get my chance to redeem myself soon.

Back at base camp we said our goodbyes. Soldiers in my unit were going up to Hanky and thanking him for his help. Then came the ridicule towards me. "Nunez you froze up like a bitch. You better thank your soul brother. That motherfucker knows his shit. "I didn't care that they heckled me. I was on cloud nine as they talked about Hanky. That was my big brother who kicked ass. I wanted to be just like him in the field. He displayed to me what a true hero was. I yearned to be just like that. I learned a lot that first trip in the A Shau Valley. Months later people from my unit would ask about Hanky. I walked around basecamp like I had a general star pinned on me. They'd ask for my "soul brother." That's what blacks were called in the Nam. Hanky was dark skinned like a black guy. He was a warrior built of brick, balls, and heart. It wouldn't be the last time I would see Hanky in the Nam.

The 101st Airborne Division was operating in the A Shau Valley more than most. We started into the jungle where we walked through 10 feet tall elephant grass and wait-a-minute-vines. These are vines that would snag on your uniform, rifle, etc. Also in the Nam', most soldiers carrying M-16's taped two magazines together. One would be upside down with a few inches sticking out of each side. This was to save time reloading in case we encountered a firefight. Those seconds it would save you meant the difference between living and meeting your demise. We walked staggered in 5 meter distances apart. Reason behind this was if a gook threw a frag, it wouldn't wipe out four or five of us in one shot. While looking for booby traps or tracks, my heart was racing. After 5 hours in 100+ weather and the humidity, my blouse was soaked in sweat. The weight of the 60 was horrible but it was my savior. I wouldn't let anything happen to that PIG.

After a 10-minute water break and shooting azimuths, my name was called by Sgt. Hayes. "Nunez get your ass up on point and relive PFC Boller." FAAAWWWKKKKK, I thought. Point was the worst position to be walking in the jungle. The way it goes is there is a point man. He is the first person in front of the whole squad/platoon/battalion. He is supposed to be the first one to spot the enemy, booby-traps, bunkers, etc. He is also the first one most likely to be zapped if Charlie spots him. The second person is the slack man. He's not far from the point man and also a dangerous position. But this is war. This is what it's all about. We walked through the A Shau Valley for another five hours. We set up camp on a ridge on the high ground with a 360-degree view. It was beautiful with the exception that we were in a combat zone. It reminded me of Yosemite National Park in California.

We radioed our coordinates and findings back to the CP (command post) and set up our NDP (night defense position). This required setting up claymore mines around our entire position 360-degrees. We had night watch every night and I was selected the first night. I was given the clackers for the claymores. Also I was given the starlight scope which was a telescope that had night vision. You could see daylight with it when it was pitch black in the jungles. I scanned every few minutes and shit every time I heard the wildlife make noises. Vietnam had these bullfrogs and "fuck you lizards" which sounded like they were saying "fuck you." It really messed with your mind. I didn't want to screw up or get somebody killed because of my stupidity. I stayed up wide-eyed until my shift was up. It finally ended at 0130 hours. I laid down, pulled my poncho over my head, and tried to fall asleep on the jungle floor. The monsoon rain then started. Thanks a lot Charlie.

The next day was a bit of the same. Walking through thick vegetation, sweating like a dog, calling in coordinates during our sitrep (situation report), and setting up camp in a safe spot. I had fire watch again so I remembered to stay alert and to stay alive. The next morning it was sunny and scorching already. Then came the rain again. It's hot and sunny yet its pouring!!! I had never seen weather like this ever. Sometimes war can be filled with action but the down time sometimes is torture. It really is.

We saddled up and started working our way in the A Shau. It was 0900 hours and saw our point man PFC Boller stop. He knelt down and used the fist signal which meant to stop in place. The adrenaline started pumping as we laid down waiting for the next thing to happen. I could smell marijuana in the air. I knew it wasn't us. I knew it was Charlie out there blowing grass. Sgt. Hayes went up to Boller and looked back smirking. He motioned for me to come to the front. He told me to look down the hill at my eleven o'clock. Two hundred meters away, I could see about 20 NVA soldiers. They were cooking breakfast and smoking grass. You could smell this distinct aroma. I was later told it was called "armpit sauce." It was a foul smelling fish sauce the gooks used called "nuoc mam."

They were way too relaxed and none of them were on watch. None had their rifles in hand. This was their backyard after all. They were in an open area with minimal cover. Sgt. Hayes told me once artillery rounds started hitting on them, start firing from right to left. That way I'd hit everything in the bullet path. It would also make them run into the tree line to their left. Sgt. Hayes and a few others would be waiting for the stragglers who didn't get zapped on the initial blasts. I set up my bi-pod, had my asst. gunner (PFC Whitman) next to me ready to feed me ammo, and waited. Sgt. Hayes had our RTO call in the coordinates to the "red legs" (artillery) and disappeared to our left flank. In less than a minute, 155mm artillery rounds started impacting on Charlie. 100% dead ACCURATE!!!!

I witnessed six NVA bodies fly in the air split into pieces. The others were all jacked from the artillery rounds. I saw movement and immediately opened fire as did the rest. We fired rapidly and with precision. I only saw one that ran towards Sgt. Hayes position. He'd gotten away and I was pissed. I could see in slow motion my rounds impacting into the NVA's chests, heads, and legs. It shredded them to pieces. The lone survivor didn't make it too far. The BOOM BOOM BOOM sound of Sgt. Hayes's shotgun confirmed he'd killed the straggler. We retreated, called in the fastmovers to blanket the area with napalm, and fled into the jungle. What a RUSH!!!

We double timed it to our evacuation point as our RTO (radio telephone operator) called for a pickup at our designated rally point. Within thirty minutes we heard the sounds of the "egg beaters" (UH-1 Hueys) coming in. We loaded on fast and lifted off. We got to basecamp and headed straight for the field showers. After that, it was off to the E club (enlisted mens club) to break out ice cold beer and very high grade grass. We got loaded till the wee hours while listening to music like Jimi Hendrix, the Doors, and the Four Tops. I loved hearing Buffalo Springfield's "For what it's worth" or Jefferson Airplane's "White Rabbit" as I smoked a joint. I was still on a high I can't convey enough. Killing didn't mean shit to me. I was proud I did good. I wanted more. It was addicting.

I woke up the next morning feeling like trash. I drank way too much and smoked way too much grass. So once I woke up, I lit up another joint and went to see what was going on in base camp. At LZ Sally, some soldiers had put up a volleyball net and there was an exciting game going on. Some soldiers were at the PX stocking up on the latest goodies and girlie magazines. I asked Sgt. Hayes when we were going back in the field. He said a few days. He was talking about going to town later and if I wanted to go. I said sure and chilled in my cot writing letters till the afternoon. Also fighting off the relentless wave of mosquitos.

A group of us soldiers ended up going to this small village/town down Highway 1 about five miles away from basecamp. Obviously the vets in country longer than us cherries had been here before. The little village was littered with all kinds of children running around and playing. It didn't even seem like they knew a war was going on but they did. One valuable thing I learned was the children in these villages knew where all the booby-traps were. They'd avoid certain areas like the plague. I kept that one in my pocket and never got careless when we were sweeping vils. Another thing I realized was a lot of the locals had black colored teeth. This was from them chewing a plant called betel nut. It was supposed to give them a buzz and keep them awake for long periods of time.

The bathhouses were one of a kind. That's a better name than a whorehouse. Vietnamese hookers would come out and all say they were numbah one. There were beaucoup (a lot) women there and they were so damn gorgeous. When the French were in Vietnam fighting years before, they had mixed with the local Vietnamese. The French-Vietnamese mixture had made them even more beautiful. We called these "round-eyes." I'm telling you these women were HOT!! Wearing those sexy Ao-Dai's (flowing robes) you could see through the fabric the sexy bodies of these women. After bargaining a price with mamasan (the oldest lady of the whorehouse and usually the ugliest), we all went in and picked our woman for the evening. We would first get bathed in a Jacuzzi style hot tub. All the crud and dirt came off of us as we were scrubbed like kings. We drank American beer and had sex till we were almost dead. Once we were all done, it was back to basecamp.

We were back in the field once again and operating in the A Shau Valley. Earlier in the week, a company from another unit had ran into an NVA buzzsaw. The gooks were geniuses at setting up "L" or "U" shaped ambushes. It created mass confusion and friendly fire killing. We looked to get as many KIA's (killed in action) as possible. We were just about finished after a week in the A Shau. Suddenly the whole jungle erupted in fire. The echoing sound of the enemy AK-47's "BLAAAAP BLAAAAP BLAAAAP" fire sent us on the deck. Rounds were whistling and cracking in the earth around us. I was so scared I pissed my pants. I'm not even embarrassed to admit that. I rose up and secured a safe firing spot near a huge boulder. I started laying down cover fire and heard a few gooks scream in agony. I knew I was on target and kept firing. PFC Whitman kept my 60 fed. More fire started coming my way and the RPG rockets started impacting near our position. Whitman and I had perfect cover so a lot of shrapnel was deflected from this. It saved our asses. The firefight lasted 30 minutes or so. All of a sudden someone said "PUFF n SPOOKY" were here. These were nicknames giving to AC-47 gunships firing miniguns, rockets, and flares. It looked like a dragon spitting out fire. You came to love hearing they were in our skies protecting us when shit hit the fan. After a few minutes it was all silence.

Then as we neared the medic station set up in the rear, we saw lifeless GI bodies. We'd suffered four casualties according to our medic Doc Willis. The estimated enemy KIA count was 35. Many others were dragged out by fish hooks by their comrades. The gooks never left their dead behind. They'd always come back for them. Seeing my deceased friends now laying in OD green body bags pissed me the fuck off. My fear had turned to anger. I wanted to waste as many of these motherfuckers as I could. I have my chance real soon. My fear of the "bush" turned into a love for it. I couldn't wait to get back in there and inflict damage to the tenth power. I was loving the jungle, loving the war. I belonged in Vietnam for sure. I could even smell the gooks when they were close. Other soldiers started recognizing this. They started calling me "The BLOODHOUND."

I'd been in country for almost two and a half months. I'd done good in the many firefights we'd encountered and became reliable under heavy enemy fire. I didn't care too much about my days I had in country. What I did count was the time I hit 180 days. This meant I'd get a week off of R&R (rest and relaxation) to a neighboring country. GI's went to either Hawaii, Thailand, or Australia. Married guys went to Hawaii. I knew I'd be going to Bangkok, Thailand. All I had to reach was 180 days. That itself was a feat. I prayed I'd make it. I heard a ton of good stories about Bangkok.

Chapter 9: On the Road to 180

LZ Sally was our home away from home. It was now November of 1968. Thanksgiving was two weeks away and we'd still get rocket attacks almost weekly. They always came at the most perfect time when you finally were relaxing or just lost in your own thoughts. One thing I witnessed a lot of was the bad press on the war back home. We'd get articles of what was going on back in the world and newspapers sent from back home. There were all kinds of protests throughout the US and college campuses. We were listening to the radio when they announced "The Fish Cheer." Here's the opening verse.

"C'mon all you big strong men,

Uncle Sam needs your help again.

He's got himself in a terrible jam,

Way done under in Viet-NAM.

So put down your books and pick up a gun,

We're gonna have a whole lot of fun.

And it's 1-2-3 what are we fighting for?

Don't ask me I don't give a damn,

My next stop is Viet-NAM.

And its 5-6-7 open up the pearly gates.

Well there ain't no time to wonder why,

WHOOPIE!! We're all gonna die."

Songs like this one by Country Joe and the Fish echoed through the US. I actually found it quite amusing. It was nice of these drug-induced students sitting in college without a care in the world. They never appreciated what we were doing over in Nam. If it wasn't for people like myself and others, they'd be in the jungles with us. Fuck them anyways. Ungrateful fuckers I thought. Seemed like the majority of it was coming from San Francisco. Hence the hippie movement was in full effect: Peace, Love, Drugs. People wearing tie dyed shirts and bandanas. They'd be calling Vietnam Veterans "baby killers" and shit like that. It made my blood boil and now ex-Vietnam vets were among the protesters. I wanted no part of that and didn't care to read about this kind of crap.

I was in Vietnam fighting for my country as were many more. Vietnam was my world for now. I concentrated solely on it for the most part to stay frosty in the bush. I saw before soldiers who concentrated too much on their life back in the world. They usually got zapped or performed like shit in the bush. We didn't need any mistakes like that when you're in the A Shau Valley. Also some guys would receive a "Dear John" letter and lose it. This is a letter from their girlfriend or wife saying it was over. Then came the joke about "Jody." Jody was the name for a man who'd stolen your girl back home. I never gave a damn about that. Plus, there were a ton of gorgeous Vietnamese women here closer to us than our own. The way I saw it was I'd deal with that type of stuff when I got back to the world. Whenever that day would be.

Things had changed around basecamp quite a bit. Sgt. Hayes and Lt Marks had rotated back to the world. It was their time to go. It was great to see them happy about going home. Our new platoon sergeant was a black bodybuilder looking guy named Sgt. Townsend. He was from Dayton, Ohio. Our new LT was a white guy named Lt. West. He was from Kissimmee, Florida and was a semi-pro tennis player before entering the Army. He was also a West Point graduate. Both were seasoned veterans and knew the country well. Also we started getting a few "cowboys" on our team. That's what we called the local Montagnard guys. They were village people who were just as smart as the VC and NVA. I loved having them out in the bush with us. We all learned a lot from them and they could spot booby-traps miles away. Also they spoke the language very well and could spot undercover VC's in vils we were sweeping through. Tough SOB's.

We began operating in different parts of I Corps conducting many search and destroy missions. We also were getting into intense firefights especially in the A Shau Valley. It seemed like the gooks were amping up their attacks. Even when we were at LZ Sally, we'd have to call for arty outside the wire in basecamp from Firebases Bastogne, Jack, Birmingham, or Veghel to stop the gooks. They starting hitting US bases with "human wave attacks." These were just vicious and nonstop attacks that kept coming at us one wave at a time. Good thing for arty, fastmovers, PUFF, and SPOOKY. You could see when they attacked us with all the green tracers from the enemy flying in our direction. Then you'd see our red tracers firing back. It looked like a space ship war type of scene. Some STAR WARS type of some sorts perhaps.

I had grown real close to a soldier who came in five days after I did. His name was PFC Mendez and he was from Tucson, Arizona. He was half Mexican-half Hopi Indian. He was a real character and always had a joke for us. We'd go to the E-club together in between missions and smoke grass. Sgt. Townsend would come out and smoke with us too. I loved the fact that everyone around us were close knit. We had to depend on each other in order to stay alive. Mendez became my best friend in Nam.

Some people I met in Nam were some of the best. The most brave, heartless, and funniest of the world. I'll try to tell you about the ones that stick out the most. One in particular was a black soldier named PFC "Doo-Dirty." I can't remember his real name. We went by nicknames or last names in Nam. He was a country boy from North Carolina. He loved marijuana too. He was the "soul" of the company. Whether we were in a firefight or back at basecamp, he'd be uplifting us in ways you couldn't imagine. He had hair that looked like Buckwheat from the Little Rascals. His voice was a carbon copy of the famous actor Chris Rock. He was never in a bad mood. He wouldn't let the company's morale fall in the pits. EVER. He had three months to finish his tour. On one patrol in January 1969, we were hit hard by a Sapper Battalion east of Hue. Charlie had his shit together that day. Doo-Dirty caught an enemy RPG round straight to the cranium. He was decapitated and killed instantly. That day it felt like the whole company died. We inflicted damage like no other after that. He was the heart and soul of LZ Sally. His voice alone would draw crowds. He was a walking comedy show. He was our dude. Talking about special people like "Doo-Dirty" still rock my soul. It still hurts. He never knew how important he was to us!!!!!

Another guy that sticks out is a dude we called "Combat Jones." He was a white boy from Bozeman, Montana. This motherfucker was a savage. I mean a straight nut job. He loved wasting gooks more than he loved life. Nobody would fuck with this guy. He'd volunteer to walk point constantly in hopes he'd meet Charlie face first. At night while we had our NDP (night defense perimeter) and claymores set, he'd wake us up. "I'll be back. Going outside to hunt me some gook meat." He would go outside of our NDP and go solo hunting in the jungle.

The worst part was he usually came back screaming "they're behind me. "He'd whack a few gooks and would wake up their buddies. Then we'd have to call for arty and extraction. He'd compromise our position. After a few times of this shit, Sgt. Townsend warned him. "Jones you go outside our fuckin perimeter at night one more time, I'll frag your ass myself. You understand me? You sick son of a bitch." Jones responded "Crystal clear Sergeant." That guy had issues. He was great under fire though. I will say that. He'd carry a necklace of gook ears in his rucksack. You catch my drift?

The weather was nuts and still raining hard. There was mud everywhere. It made it even harder for the deuce and a halves to drive in the thick red clay earth. We had one more mission to go on before Thanksgiving. We were inserted to an area where intel had reported seeing enemy movement. We went over our maps as soon as we got to the tree line. Something was terribly wrong. I let Mendez know to stay alert as we were walking through the jungle. It was at night and almost pitch black. I told my AG Whitman to be ready. They were around here and close. I could smell them. Sgt. Townsend told the RTO to call for illumination rounds to our direct front. Illumination rounds were rounds that popped over the intended targets and lit up that whole area with a small white parachute attached. Once the illumination rounds hit, we could see damn near a whole company of NVA soldiers walking slowly. We opened up on them and they returned fire. RTO called for "fire for effect" on our same coordinates and arty started impacting with devastation. The CRUUUMP CRUUUMP CRUUUMP sounds were shaking the earth and we kept up all the fire. We were so close a gook threw a Chi-com grenade at our position.

Whitman quickly picked it up and threw it back towards the gook, blowing him in shreds instantly killing him. Wow, this was crazy yet a rush. This mission we suffered a few WIA's (wounded in action) but no casualties. Our most serious was a young soldier who stepped on a toe popper. Too young to lose a foot. Made me angrier. This time we caught an NVA soldier as a POW (prisoner of war). He had gunshot wounds in both legs. We took him with us for medical attention and then interrogation. We'd let the cowboys handle the interrogation. They usually got the enemy soldiers to crack and give up information freely after some TLC.

Thanksgiving was actually a nice event at basecamp. I think most of us had our turkey dinner and reminisced about our families back home. Some of us got mail from the states and opened it up. The meal was great and there was a black and white television playing in the chow hall. Someone had received Christmas lights in a care package and strung them up throughout the basecamp. I heard that there was a card game going on in the bunker near the E club. The bunker was an underground type hidden area built for partying. I was all up for it. Everyone who had liquor and dope took it to the party. I was also a good card player so I was ready to make some money.

Before we went to the party, Mendez and I took our dirty laundry to a mamasan who washed GI clothes for MPC's. These were military payment certificates that we were paid with. We called it "funny money" since they looked like monopoly money. They could be redeemed for money but not for US currency. It could be redeemed for Dong (Vietnamese dollars). This prevented a wave of US currency flowing wild in Vietnam. We dropped by the PX and headed out to the bunker. Let the party begin. I couldn't wait. We didn't have to go back to the field till Monday so we had plenty of time to recover. I would spend the remainder of my weekend writing letters home, cleaning my 60, and listening to music while drinking some beers. When I'd write letters back home you never let your family know you were in danger. You played it off like it was nothing and happy times. I knew Mom and Dad wouldn't buy it. It's not like they sent us to band camp, lol. We were in WAR.

The Ho Chi Minh trail went all the way down from Laos to Cambodia and would slip into Vietnam as their key supply routes. The NVA thought as long as they weren't seen in other countries that we wouldn't bomb them in Cambodia or Laos. Yeah right, they found out otherwise. B-52's to bird dogs would drop ordinance all over the Ho Chi Minh trail. It would disrupt their ability to transport weapons and supplies to the field. The Soviet Union were supplying the Communist North Vietnamese while we supplied the South Vietnamese army. They were the ARVN (Army of Republic of Vietnam). We called them "Marvin the ARVN" and they'd go out in the bush with us too. The only problem I had with some of the ARVN's was they talked too damn loud. I didn't to get my shit blown in the wind cause of these retards. We had the cowboys shut them up. It worked.

The strangest things occur in war. You hear of stories that are almost impossible to believe. One in particular stands out more than the rest. Sometime in the first week of December we were on patrol near the south end of the A Shau Valley. We had been out in the field for a week and a half. We'd made contact with Charlie three times. That was three times too many. We humped up on a ridge and had a clear view of the valley. We had supreme cover up there. We were taking a break. It was baking hot as usual.

Lt. West came up. "Nunez, collect all the canteens and leave your 60 here. Take that FNG PFC Sam with you. He will provide cover for you in case you run into a dink. There's a stream we passed about two hundred meters down the ridge. Get water for us. Hurry back." Sam and I go down to the stream. I had my 45 pistol with me in my side holster. Sam was supposed to be providing cover for me. As I was filling up canteens, I saw a large ripple coming from the east end of the stream. I looked up and shit a brick. No more than 30 meters away stood three Viet Cong soldiers. They had just crossed the stream. They were just as shocked to see us there. They were dressed in black pajamas. They all wore Non-La's. They all had AK-47's pointed at us. We were dead!!!

I was wondering why Sam hadn't opened up on these bastards. I turned to see where he was at. He had his rifle a few feet away from him. His boots were off and he'd been washing his feet. UNBELIEVABLE!!!! Some cover huh? I stood up and locked eyes at the smallest VC closest to me. What seemed like an hour was only about 15 seconds. I waited to see the muzzle flash and the rounds impact into my body. I prayed and said goodbye. The next thing I know, the three VC's crossed the stream and disappeared into the elephant grass. I couldn't believe it!!!!! We gathered ourselves quickly and headed up the ridge. I told Sam we weren't going to say shit about it. He agreed since he knew it would be his ass. He'd dropped the ball providing security. I told him if he said a word I'd whack his ass myself. The secret was ours forever-up until today.

My thoughts on this was simple. In war, sometimes you become battle-weary. You just don't want to make contact sometimes. The VC had probably known there was more of us. Had they zapped Sam and I near the stream, our company would've been alerted. They'd have artillery, napalm, and hellfire sailing their way by the truckload. They probably just wanted peace for a day. I'm glad it was the day we dropped our guard. God watching over me as always. A true miracle there.

Patrols had been going on in I Corps all month of December. It was like chasing ghosts in the dense jungle. I sometimes felt like they had cameras out there watching our every move. Anyhow, we'd make contact with a few gooks popping out of tree lines and spider holes but nothing major. It was like the C&C (command and control) were taking it easy this month. We weren't hitting as much enemy. On December 17th 1968 we went out on patrol in the A Shau Valley. We were dropped off by Hueys and set up perimeter. We started making contact and enemy mortars started raining in on our positions. We all started laying fire downwind and called for an immediate extraction. We had run into the 9th NVA Regiment and its bunker complexes. They were well dug in and had multiple rocket teams firing on us. We called in everything from arty to naval gunships. They blew the NVA to pieces but still were too dug in to exterminate them all. We all set up and loaded on as

Hueys came in to our LZ to get us. A B-52 ("carpet bombing") strike was immediately ordered on the enemy position as well as arty and naval gunships. God I could only imagine the pounding they would be receiving. I knew we'd be back soon to see how much damage we'd inflicted on them.

We could see LZ Sally in a distance and it was all smiles throughout our helos. If you ever want to see a happy soldier, watch him as he comes back from a combat firefight. Once inside the wire, he feels protected and safe. You could see the happiness and joy on his face. I'll never forget that feeling or that look. I'm sure I made it myself many times. I could feel my face breaking once we could see our helopads. It was our home and our safety.

Mendez and Whitman came up to me. They said they had a nice bottle of liquor from the states. Southern Comfort I believe it was. "So-Co" as it was called. Damn that stuff was strong!!!! I still can't drink that to this day. Anyways we went to the bunker and were met outside by other soldiers from our unit. There was a full on BBQ going and case upon case of beer. Mendez then tells me how we just two months till our 180 days. R&R was coming up. I told him not to jinx it. He told me he'd be going a week after me. I told him I was going to Bangkok. He told me he was going to Australia. I hadn't thought that time had passed so fast. I was already in country for four months and was loving the bush. As long as I had my 60 I felt good. Even though we had some hair raising firefights we'd done pretty good. I hated casualties that occurred but that was a part of war. It was the ugly face of combat.

For a few months now, intel had been talking another a country wide attack. It was supposed to happen on Tet. Tet was the Vietnamese equivalent of New Years, Fourth of July, and Christmas all rolled into one. Intel was reporting that it had received multiple info about Charlie attacking every major US base in Vietnam. It would be another "Tet Offensive." Commanding generals had different opinions of whether it would happen or not. We would soon find out who was right and who was wrong.

Christmas came and it was a nice little celebration in basecamp. We had a Christmas tree with empty beer cans as ornaments tied together by commo wire. Also a few real ornaments that were donated by fellow soldiers. A lot of partying in between. I was one that felt downtime was sometimes hell since boredom became your worse enemy. It was all part of the game. Plus, I had received a great care package from home with everything from candy to cookies. I sent Mom a letter and asked her to send me a sweater. It got cold at night in the jungle. I hope she would send me one. I shared my package with my brothers. We all did that. I'd read letters I'd received from home so those who didn't receive mail could hear ours. The next thing to look forward to was New Years. It would be 1969 soon. I didn't know this year would be the most brutal. Not only to me but to my personal family. If I only knew. I could see Bangkok on my horizon. I lit a joint and spun into a haze of calm. Los Bravos' "black is black" was playing as I passed out on my cot. I forgot to put my poncho over my head. I was the mosquitos' dinner that night.

Chapter 10: W.I.A. (2/13/69)

1969 came with a bang. We had been on a few missions that we hair raising. It seemed that every time we went out on patrol we'd get run into Charlie. He was usually with a lot of his friends and it was getting more intense. By this time, I was really in tuned with the terrain and its lovely booby-traps Charlie would leave for us. I was so comfortable in the bush that I rather be there than basecamp. I felt invincible and wanted to unleash havoc on these little bastards. The thing that kept me fresh out there was the fact that I'd stared death in the face for almost five months. I walked with the devil in this hell called Vietnam. I'd kill him too if he dared show his face. As I stated earlier, walking point was the most dangerous position in the bush. I rarely walked point since I carried the 60. I was usually in the center of the squad.

After about a month of serious patrolling the A Shau and its surrounding areas, we'd taken a week break. The Tet Offensive was fresh in the minds of our leaders. They were thinking that perhaps it could actually be good intel. It sure did. Tet is Vietnam's New Year around end of January. The VC and NVA surrounded and trapped Marines. Both in the cities of Khe Sanh and Hue. It took basically two months of animalistic fighting but the Marines held their ground. We took back the cities and airstrips from the NVA. We were to be on HIGH alert for attacks on every basecamp or firebase. We got attacked night and day for two weeks. It was horrendous. It was the peak of Tet continuing from 68'. We would be sent out in the A Shau Valley to flush a lot of these bastards out. We started going out in the neighboring Ruong Ruong Valley also. We experienced intense firefights over the next two weeks. This year the gooks wouldn't be good boys and stay home partying. It would last for a while even after I left wounded. They'd make up for lost time in a quick way. After Tet was over, the Viet Cong was irrelevant for the remainder of the war.

Back after the firefight, things at LZ Sally were pretty on edge. We'd had no good down time after being on alert for a whole week. There were no BBQ's going and the no music was blaring throughout basecamp. We hadn't gone down to the local bathhouses in a while. I had heard my brother Hanky was in a town called Phu Bai. I was hoping to see him soon. It was a longshot but what the hell I would be nice to have some family around.

The next day we were told to all meet in the chow hall for a briefing from our Colonel. Colonel Wilson was a lifer who had built his career in wars before. He had a great record. He had medals from World War II and the Korean War. There was a big map on the board where every soldier could see. Intel had reported that we'd be working some areas in the West end of the A Shau Valley. The flyboys had surveillance photos of well dug in complexes at the tops of some hills especially around and near Dong Ap Bia. Three months later, this would be the site of the ferocious battle named "Hamburger Hill." We would be operating around those areas and would clear these areas out before reaching our objective. The estimated time to complete our total sweep would be around four months. Other units would be operating to the North and South of us. It would take this long due to the area highly saturated with NVA regular, trucks, equipment, and mortars. One thing the gooks also had was anti-aircraft missiles and firepower strong enough to knock out a fastmover or a helo out of the sky.

We were inserted to an area around 1700 hours on February 9th 1969. It was a whole company of us this time. This consisted of four platoons (around 180 troops) on the ground. The objective was to work west and eliminate any enemy complexes or bunkers along the way. We started humping through the hills and its rugged terrain. The A Shau Valley was the devil's playground. I had a feeling we'd be meeting Charlie on this trip. Perhaps more than once.

We'd be out in the field for a week and then back to basecamp. Once we got back, I'd get my shit packed and two days later I'd be on my flight to Bangkok for a week. I was going to have the time of my life there. There would be no war there. Only girls, booze, and drugs. I could surely use the rest and relaxation. I couldn't wait.

February 12th 1969 was spent patrolling in the A Shau Valley. It was a warm humid day. Surprisingly we hadn't hit any heavy enemy contact as expected. Then again intel sucked and was like a crap shoot. But in the A Shau it usually was dead on. This concerned a lot of us since we knew there would be a lot of them there. Why we weren't attacked was not the norm. We'd been in some firefights that maybe lasted a minute but nothing big. Also today it was my 20th birthday. We lit up a joint that night and prayed the next four days would go smooth. The next day would be hell on earth. It would also be my last day fighting in Vietnam.

It was a Thursday, February 13th 1969. This day would be etched in my life forever. We were patrolling a dense jungle area in the A Shau Valley. It was a clear morning. Around 1100 hours, once we came down a bend in the jungle all hell erupted. We had run into an NVA regiment as intel had said. There were bunkers all over and we were in a shitty spot. We started to go to high ground and take cover. Rockets started impacting our area as I started getting the 60 kicking. The barrage of rounds coming my way made Whitman and I move to a more elevated spot. We started in on the enemy immediately. We heard constant screams of pain and agony echoed on both sides. Enemy Chi-Com grenades stared impacting around us. One of our guys started shooting the "thump-gun" (M-79 grenade launcher) in the enemy bunkers. It was making a difference. Our RTO started calling for gunships and arty. This was the million-dollar moment and rounds were impacting all around us. I was firing and wasting as many as I could. I then saw PFC Mendez go down. He was my best friend in Vietnam and I was going to rescue him. I left our position and went to pull him out of harm's way. A rocket impacted right besides knocking us both on our asses. My ears were ringing yet I regained composure and my 60. I started laying down cover fire and pulling Mendez out at the same time. I laid enough fire power down range for a few others to pull out more wounded soldiers. They'd been on the point element. Then felt like I'd been punched in the back and shoulder area. I'd taken an enemy round from an AK-47. Right in the back.

In that instant I saw an NVA soldier shooting my way. I aimed my 60 and shredded that motherfucker. I hadn't even realized I'd been shot till then. I was still dragging Mendez and collapsed when we reached cover behind some boulders. I called for a "MEDIC" and once Doc arrived he started dragging Mendez towards the rear to be worked on. He was in bad shape and it didn't look good. I became angrier than I ever had and rose up with my 60 blasting towards the enemy. As I rose up, I felt my lower back shattering and fell into the ground face first. I could feel my lungs filling with blood. I could taste that nastiness. My whole blouse was soaked with blood. I would find out later that Lt. West had panicked and accidentally shot me two times above the ass. Also, I was simultaneously hit again by an enemy round. This time I was hit in the collarbone area. I never faulted Lt. West for that. War was hell and chaos. I knew it was a mistake and I hope it didn't haunt him throughout life.

The next thing I know was I was being patched up by our medic. I felt weak and for the first time I thought I might die right there in the jungles of Nam'. I quickly got rid of that thought and told myself I was going to live no matter what. They started an IV on me and I was slipping in and out of consciousness. Once the IV started, I felt more alert and more alive. I couldn't move and pain had immersed my whole body. The fighting kept on going and our RTO called for a medevac helo. The request kept getting denied due to the heavy gunfire they were getting while making gun runs over our position. They had called in for everything we had on our enemy positions. That meant naval gunships, arty, SPOOKY, PUFF, and fastmovers. The impacting firepower was so close we could feel the heat coming off from the impact areas. Once it was clear the first Huey dropped a "jungle penetrator" down. There wasn't enough clearing for an LZ. Plus, it was too dangerous. So a jungle penetrator was lowered. This was a stretcher dropped down to pull critically wounded out of a hot zone. While waiting to be loaded on I heard Doc say "only the WIA's (wounded in action) on this one." I weakly asked Doc "Mendez ok?" He shook his head and said "KIA." My heart hurt even more. I was laid on another soldier and lifted out of the air. He was KIA.

As we were being airlifted out of the jungle I could feel the soldier underneath me getting hit by enemy fire. I knew I was next. I peeked down for a quick second. I could see NVA soldiers all pointing their weapons in my direction. They began to fire. Then the cobra gunships made a pass and destroyed them in one volley of fire. Enemy limbs went flying all over. I wanted to get in the helo and get in NOW. When we reached the helo we were immediately pulled in. The medics on the helo laid us both down. I heard one saying the other soldier was KIA (killed in action). His body saved my life basically. Doc knew what he was doing. Our Medics were our saviors in the bush. Hands down. The medics started concentrating on me since I was the only one alive. I could feel the air hitting my head and wondering how bad I was wounded. I hoped I could walk again let alone live normal again. All I know was this: I was headed to a hospital in Phu Bai.

I was told I would be going home with these wounds by the medics. I couldn't believe it. One day after my 20th birthday and my war was over in Vietnam. My 60 was gone, frags gone, and my best friend gone. My chains of linked 7.62 ammo were gone. No OD green "drive on towel" around my neck either. I felt naked. I was crushed. I still wondered if maybe I made a full recovery I would be able to return to my unit. I had unfinished business with Charlie. Deep down inside I knew I'd never see Vietnam again.

I ended up at a hospital in Phu Bai and they immediately lead me into surgery. There were other soldiers in there screaming and crying in pain. Two things you will always hear from a wounded grown man: God or Mother. I never screamed for either surprisingly. I guess the adrenaline had me wired. Hell I didn't even know I was wounded the first time. Come to find out I'd been hit by one round in my back and two above my ass. I could see all these nurses and doctors running around me and calling for different medical instruments. A chaplain was going around reading "last rites" to the mortally wounded. I could see panic in some of their faces but I remained calm. I didn't want to die of shock. I had tubes in my mouth, back, and shoulder. I could see blood being drained out of my lung. I started praying to God that he'd spare me and let me live. I felt a sense of peace after I prayed. An overwhelming peaceful took over me. I laid there on the hospital operating table frozen. My war was over for good. At least I thought so at that time.

While recovering a few days later in the hospital in Phu Bai, I seen a medical staff come into my room. Also my back would require need extensive patching up. I was not paralyzed but would need a substantial amount of recovery time. I would be sent to Da Nang where I'd get a flight to Japan. There my recovery would begin. I wasn't too happy about that but what choice did I have.

A few hours later I got the greatest gift I'd get in Vietnam. My brother Hanky came to visit me once again. He was on his 2nd tour in Vietnam and found out I was wounded. He came to see me before I headed to Da Nang the next day. What an uplifting reward to me. I could see it hurt him to see me all laid up. I'm sure he got payback for me. He then told me "I heard you pulled a few guys out of danger and charged two machine gun nests. You're a fuckin hero. John Wayne style!!! They say they're putting you up for the SILVER STAR. One bad ass motherfucker you are brother." I was still in drug-land and really didn't catch the medal part. Morphine was the ticket. It had me spinning.

We talked for a little while. He then told me he had to catch a ride back to basecamp. He hugged me and wished me well. Before walking out, he stopped in his tracks. He turned to me smirking and said "Mom's going to be pissed at you." He waved goodbye.

The next day I was transported to Da Nang airbase. I was still in a hospital bed and would be flying as such. We were loaded on the tarmac and locked in place. I had been given morphine but was still in extreme pain. I could feel the plane moving and once we were airborne I dozed off due to the effects of the morphine. I was leaving Vietnam forever and now going to Japan to recover. I was sad to leave but knew it was over. So I thought.

Chapter 11: Japan

I was in extreme pain and recovering in a military hospital in Tokyo, Japan. I was bedridden and had already two surgeries. I can't even remember how many stitches I received bit I know it was a lot. Like I said, I had a few more surgeries lined up in the next week depending on my healing. If I coughed my whole body lit up in pain. Same thing for sneezing and laughing. I wasn't laughing much but damn it was a bitch. The nurses would come over and give me a daily sponge bath which I didn't mind at all. I was able to eat on my own but with all the drugs being pumped into my body I lost my appetite. I wasn't eating much. There were just a lot of shock I was still in. There was a lot of things racing through my mind. Was I ever going to be the same again? Was I ever going to fully recover from all this? A lot of these things were racing through my mind.

About a week and a half later, I received a letter that shook me even more. My sister Juanita shot me a letter. It said that both my older brothers Nacho and Cirilo had joined the Army. Cirilo was already in Fort Ord and Nacho was leaving at the end of the week to Ord as well. My younger brother Ruben Spring would follow a few years later. I had to sit down. I just couldn't believe it. But hey I couldn't blame them. Their brother had been wounded in Vietnam. They wanted some freakin payback. Nacho was married and had a small daughter at the time. Yet they didn't even blink. They told Mary before they left that they'd be going to Vietnam as soon as training was completed. Nacho and Cirilo would end up leaving around the same time. Nacho went on to jump school.

By now the war protests had become a nightly show at the hospital. Every television set showed more protests throughout the country. Even the news reporters got involved in all the politics. I can remember Cronkite saying that the war was now unwinnable. Fuck them, they didn't know shit. They'd try to come and implant themselves in our company to go out on patrol once in a while. Sorry about that!! We wouldn't let them in. If they wanted to be in Vietnam, they better get in the bush and stay there for a year like the rest of us. I'd heard reporters who went out on patrol with certain units. Not only were they reportedly a pain in the ass, but they often got killed or wounded for being stupid.

The whole recovery process was slow going and not fun at all. I couldn't sneak away from the hospital or go drinking in the local bars in Tokyo. That changed my last two days there. I went to whorehouses in Tokyo with tubes sticking out of my back. I didn't give a shit. Anything beat lying in bed all day hearing other wounded vets wince and cry in pain. I wasn't sleeping either and was having recurring nightmares about February 13th. I just couldn't shut it off and it was just too much. I usually would go out on the emergency stairwell and blast a joint to calm me down. It wasn't the same after a while though. What I mean was that wouldn't work after a while. The nightmares were caused more anguish and agony. I wish I could just go to sleep and forget about it all. Of course it didn't go that way.

I was in Japan still and getting most of my feeling back especially in my shoulder area. My back still ached like crazy and it was painful to walk but I did. I could walk normal just a lot of pain that went with it. At least I still had that privilege. Over at the hospital they started having group sessions with other vets to help them cope with their wounds. Yeah no thanks. I didn't care to be in one of those groups. I didn't want to hear that.

I received a letter from my brother Nacho while he was in boot camp in Fort Ord. He was telling me that he was going to jump school after he got done with boot camp then he was putting in for Vietnam. He said in the letter Cirilo was going to go to Vietnam. Right after he got done with training at Fort Benning in Georgia. I wrote him back and wished him well. I told him to learn everything he could from the seasoned vets and he'd be fine. I had made it 6 months in the jungles of Vietnam. I was proud that I had made it so far in a harsh environment and was happy I gave it my all. Now I prayed my brothers would be okay once they landed in Vietnam.

Out of all people I'd run into in Japan, it was "Combat Jones." He'd been wounded in that nasty firefight that got me the million-dollar wound. He'd taken three rounds from an AK-47. One on the left arm, one in the left thigh, and one in his right calf. His war was over as well. When he saw me he lit up. "Hey Nunez, what's up bro? Ain't this a bitch. I want to go to Vietnam. But they say I'm going back to the world. I got a plan. Let's steal weapons from the armory. We'll go and whack these Jap motherfuckers since we can't get back to Nam. What you think of my master plan?" I shook my head and told him to go to bed. Jones wouldn't be going home. His plans were derailed when a psych doctor interviewed him. He was on his way to a psychiatric hospital back in the world. There were guys like Jones that were in the bush too long. Or had seen too much. Their heads were fried. He was one of them.

Things went like clockwork for the next two months. Medical tests went on and the changing of bandages and tubes were a daily ritual for me by this time. I just wanted all this shit to be over so I could rotate back to the world and get on with my life. I knew once I got back I'd go straight to Lederman hospital for more recovery. Hopefully by that time I would be done with my military time and go home. The last thing I wanted to do was to go back to Fort Bragg and waste time there. I rather go back to Nam' wounded!!!!!

By this time, two months had passed and they told me I'd be going back to the world. As I had thought, I'd be going to Lederman hospital for a few weeks. After that though it would probably be back to Bragg. Ah fawwwwwk man, I was hoping never to see that mud pile. Well it was okay I guess since I was a short timer and had less than a year to go. While I was in bed resting a Major came and pinned me with a purple heart. He said thank you for your service and some idiot took a picture of the whole thing. Probably for the military magazine" Stars and Stripes" or something like that. Those magazines were pretty cool and would tell stories about how Charlie was zapped by American forces in many ways including grotesque ones.

I was told to be ready early the next morning. I couldn't wait. I mean, Japan was a beautiful country but I wanted to be back in the States already. Enough of these hospitals and crap. I wanted to get back to my normal self, my normal routine. I was living in fantasy land thinking like that though. It was going to be a new beginning for me. I felt normal with the occasional back pain but it was getting better. I was ready for the United States. I couldn't wait to kiss the ground there. There was no place like home.

Chapter 12: Back to The World

It was end of April 1969. It was time to kiss Tokyo good-bye and rotate back to the world. I did like Japan but I was ready to leave. I needed to be in the USA. I got on a military plane among our wounded veterans. Some tried to strike up conversations with the normal bullshit questions "where'd you go in Nam' or where you in the shit?" I didn't want to sound rude but in my head I felt like screaming "I didn't get shot up behind a FUCKING desk you retard!" It would be the same reason I didn't want to go to those VFW or Vets Lodges. Every damn one of them was full of vets talking about firefights and war. Some I could tell was bullshit. I had no patience with that. It reminded me of those REMF's (rear echelon mother fuckers) that never went in the bush and never witnessed combat. Their rank saved them from that. They'd write themselves up for medals and go home telling stories of being a war hero to their families. Chickenshits!! Some would say I thought our shit didn't stink. Yeah well I had six months in the "bush" mostly in enemy beehives like the A Shau and Ruong Ruong Valleys. Some vets had much more than that. Some of us actually earned the right to be there. We were combat proven. I sat in my seat and waited as we pushed out to the runway. I smiled as I saw the Pacific Ocean underneath us and Japan out of view now. I was going home. In 12 hours we'd be landing in San Francisco, California, UNITED STATES OF AMERICA!!!!

The first thing I can vividly remember is getting off the plane at San Francisco airport. We got off the runway and walked in. We had our fatigues on which were OD green. We were proud to wear our uniforms and represent our country. We had survived in hell and were finally home. As some of us veterans walked through the concourse, we were greeted with a plethora of sneers from people there. I could see people in the airport avoid us like we were lepers. If someone was walking towards us, they immediately moved away hastily. I could hear some assholes whisper "baby-killers" and shit like that. That pissed me off and I wanted to blow their fuckin heads off. It angered me that so many people had no idea what was really going on in Vietnam. Yet they were all experts and felt like they knew more than us who'd actually been there. Believe it or not, we were there to help poverty stricken people there. We had heard overseas that Frisco was the hub of all anti-war protests. A lot of hippies wore tie-dyed shirts and bandanas. A lot of em' had shirts with slogans "Make love not war" and things like that. They were also into drugs like acid, pot, and LSD. I remember the bad taste in my mouth when I heard some idiot yell "we don't you fuckers here." I thought to myself this is my country I fought for. I deserve to be here. We'd been warned in Japan by a Sergeant about this kind of crap going on. I couldn't wait to get out the airport and get to Lederman Hospital. By the time I left the airport I felt drained. Not only that, I felt ashamed. Bashing slurs, dirty looks, and middle fingers directed at us were greetings we got from the American people. As I walked outside the airport, I lit up a cigarette and whispered to myself, "Welcome Home Jimmy." Some welcoming huh?

Those of us who were going to Lederman Hospital were to jump on a bus. Other veterans who were going home were picked up by family members or had connecting flights to catch. The bus ride was eerily quiet. We were window watching as if we had never been to America before. It was so nice to see "Old Glory" flying everywhere in sight. As soon as we pulled up to Lederman hospital we were escorted to our rooms and given our appointment schedules. These were all of our doctor and rehabilitation appointments. I looked at my schedule for the week and saw it had group therapy. Yeah I would probably be skipping that shit. To top it all off most of these doctors looked exactly like the fuckers we'd be killing for a year. Looked like Charlie's cousins!!!!! What a mindfuck!!!!! I almost strangled one of these assholes for getting smart with me. I had to be subdued by other veterans. Mind you, they were supposed to be there to help us. Not to mess with us or belittle us. I wasn't taking shit from anybody there. I met some hot orderlies working at the hospital and begin to go out for drinks with them. Women were never a problem for me and always seemed like enough to go around. I started having sex with a few of them. They'd shift my schedules to my liking and I'd get group therapy checked off as if I'd been there. This was great. While veterans went to appointments, I'd go to the movies or be at one of the blonde orderlies houses' boning them. They also liked to smoke grass which was music to my ears. They'd get the "Humboldt county" marijuana that was off the charts. You'd be high off your ass if you smoked half a joint. I still say Vietnam's marijuana was untouchable. But I wasn't going back there so this was perfect.

"NOW HERE THIS, NOW HEAR THIS. PFC SANTIAGO J NUNEZ PLEASE REPORT TO ROOM #212. ONCE AGAIN ROOM# 212." This is what my Monday morning wake-up call sounded like. I reported to room 212 and nobody was there. I sat on the chair and turned the TV on. A few minutes later Dr. Gibson walked in. He was my doctor there at Lederman and was going over my rehabilitation charts. He asked me how I was feeling and went over a few stretches. He checked my bandages on my wounds and told me the healing was going great. I told him I was still in pain but it was slowly making progress. Then he sat down and asked if could ask me a personal question. I said "sure." He replied "Do you know you are being recommended for the Silver Star?" I was confused and yet proud at the same time. I just couldn't conceive what was actually happening. Why me I thought. I didn't feel like a hero. I was just doing my job like everyone else. The medals belonged to guys like Mendez who came home in a flag draped coffin. Those were my heroes. Men who gave their all. Men who'd never see their mothers or fathers again.

Dr. Gibson said he was honored to meet a highly decorated veteran. He explained to me "not everybody gets these Nunez. You should be proud for what you did on February 13th. I read the report and transcripts. Some heart and balls you have. Congratulations Nunez. Welcome home Airborne." Now THAT was the first time anyone had told me that. I felt good hearing that. Especially since we'd been mocked and verbally bashed everywhere we went since returning to the world. Almost made you want to go back to Vietnam.

Dr. Gibson said he put in a request for me to get put on "convalescent leave." That meant I would be able to return home and recover there instead of being stuck in a hospital. It was almost like getting royal treatment. I'd be getting full pay except I wouldn't have to go back to my base. Music to my ears. It was now May of 1969 and my two older brothers were in the Army now. The draft was still going on. This is where Uncle Sam sent you a lovely letter saying you had thirty days to report for duty. Most draftees were definitely going to Vietnam. My brothers and I had volunteered to go so they never had to find us. I was just hoping our youngest brother Mike didn't get drafted. He was a loner who didn't really want to go to Vietnam.

Yet I knew if he was ever drafted, he wouldn't run like a punk to Canada or Mexico. I didn't want him going to Vietnam either.

One particular fact that we later learned was crucial. Many "Ivy League families" whose sons didn't want to go to Vietnam found a way out. Their families sent them to hide in Canada so they could attend college with no interruptions. When the Vietnam War was completely over years later, the SAME cowards asked for clemency. It was bought and they were allowed back into the United States. They are many CEO's and congressmen here today. Like the U.S. Government, most wanted the veterans of Vietnam to die off. They didn't want to hire veterans like us. It exposed them for the cowards they were. They died inside long time ago when they ran up North!!!!

I asked Dr. Gibson how long I would be on this special leave. He told me until I was fit to go back to my base and train like a regular soldier. I still had 8 months of military service owed to my favorite Uncle. I was going to heal wonderfully at home. I called Mom and Dad and told them I'd be flying home the next day. They were ecstatic and couldn't wait. I was going to be landing in Burbank airport. I was finally going home. To my real home in Pacoima on Telfair Avenue.

I flew into Burbank airport the following day. I was greeted by Dad who gave me a big hug. He wasn't the most affectionate one but I felt his love. He had tears in his eyes that he quickly wiped away. Dad was a man that was made of heart, stone, and guts. But he was a family man. He never went out to bars or nightclubs. He was always working and when not working with his family. He'd drink tequila and squirts that were so strong it was like drinking firewater. Dad was one tough man who I highly respect to this day. We jumped in his Ford van and jumped on the 5 freeway headed to Pacoima. Headed home.

We talked about how his trucking business was going and what was new. He told me Mom, Pat, Evelyn, and Bobby were waiting for me at the house. I pulled into the long driveway at our house. I saw Mom come out of the house first. She was so happy. We hugged and cried together. She told me how much she loved me and she was happy I was home. I knew she did. She didn't treat me like a foster son. I WAS her son PERIOD!!!! She treated the other foster kids there at the house just like her own. The heart and love she displayed was undisputed. I had never felt an unconditional love like this before. Not even from my own mother.

The others came out and we all hugged. We all laughed and talked about what I had missed. Basically they were filling me in about our high school friends who'd been killed in Vietnam, who'd got married, etc. Mom made a great dinner that night. We all stayed at the dinner table talking. After a while Bobby left and the girls retired to bed. Mom, Dad, and I stayed up having drinks. We had a lot to catch up on and I think we went to sleep around 4am. Two hours later I could smell Mom's coffee pot going. The aroma of fresh coffee in the house was a reminder that I was in my home. I could feel all the love and comfort here. The next thing on my list was to go see my brother Mike. He was the closest to me out of all my brothers. We'd play rough and beat the shit out of each other while growing up. It only intensified as we grew older. As usual we were still misfits. I'd heard he was working as a short order cook. It was at the Denny's restaurant off of Roxford Street near his foster parents' home. I walked in to look for Mike. The manager said he was on break. He said he usually took it behind the building. I walked around the building and spotted him sitting on a milk crate. He was reading a small bible. I whistled at him. He looked up and leaped off the milk crate. He walked fast towards me with his arms open and said "Hey Kidd you're back." We embraced and it felt so good hugging my little brother. He said how much he missed me and he loved me. I told him the same. He said he was off the next day and we should hang out together. We spent ten minutes talking about life and how he was doing. He was doing good and still thought he was Elvis and Johnny Cash. He invited me inside for a meal. I accepted his offer. I sat down and ordered a coffee. He came out from the back and introduced me to his co-workers. After my meal was finished, we said our good-byes. He promised to pick me up. The next day we'd be heading to East Los Angeles. I'd be visiting my biological Mom Bertha and my sisters Juanita and Mary. I couldn't wait.

We went to East L.A. the next day and pulled up to Boulder Street where my Mom lived. It was great to hug my Mother. I felt her love for me. She was very happy to see me as were my sisters. A lot of my cousins were there too. Mike had to go to work so he left me there and I stayed over. Mary and Juanita were there with us the whole night. I think we stayed up all the way till the next morning. They started crying at one point telling me how they thought they lost me. At that point I never really thought about how my family felt back home. Hell, I was in Vietnam. It must've been just as tough as it was for me. They'd all watch any news clipping of the war on TV hoping to see me there. What a weight that was for someone to hold. I felt guilty about that but it was part of life. We develop from our struggles and that is how strength is built. Our family had a reputation for being strong and it all started with my oldest sister Mary. She was tough and to this day she is still rockin' hard. We call her "NAILS" because she couldn't be broken. She's one tough cookie!!!!!

Now as I stated before, I was to recover at home until physically able to go back to my unit. Well I believed that would take a while, lol. I was mailed a "dream sheet" to fill out and to send back to Lederman hospital. A dream sheet is a letter from the military that asks you what's the three favorite places you'd like to be stationed at. Since I was already a Vietnam combat veteran, they would probably be keeping me close to home. That was fine by me. I listed Fort Ord as my number one. I didn't feel like going anywhere outside of California. Nor did I feel like playing wargames in the field. I hoped my last times in the military were easy. By this time, I was mentally checked out of the Army. I just wanted to be a PFC (Private Fuckin Civilian). I mailed my sheet in and forgot about that shit.

I spent the summer spending time with family and friends. I was still getting paid and living a great life. I had no time clock on me and no restrictions. I'd help out Dad with the trucks and go out at night with friends. It was perfect. Then in August I had received a certified letter saying I was to report to Lederman hospital in a week. I borrowed Dad's van and drove up there. I saw Dr. Gibson and he asked how I was doing. I bullshitted him and said I was still in pain but feeling better. He took a bunch of tests on me the next two days. After staying there for two days I couldn't wait to get my results. I had hoped he would just let me recover at home the rest of my time. By now I had five months of service left. They didn't need me in the Army. I was told on the third day I was cleared for active duty with no restrictions. Then came a blow right to the balls: I'd be going back to Fort BRAGG!!!! I told Dr. Gibson, "YOU GOT TO BE SHITTIN' ME!!!!!!!" In a week I was to report to Fort Bragg. I couldn't believe how I was going to be rotated back to this shithole after all the agony I went through to get the hell out of there. My morale went spinning down the toilet. I was going to make them pay for sending me back. I drove back to Los Angeles sicker than a dog. I vowed once I got to Bragg I'd be so defiant and uncooperative they'd just boot me out and send me back home. I wanted no part of this. Five months or not, I was going to make em' pay.

Chapter 13: Back to Bragg

Unbelievable, the next week I was heading to Fort Bragg, North Carolina. I boarded a commercial flight with all my two army duffel bags at LAX to Raleigh, North Carolina. After a 2-hour bus ride, I arrived in Fort Bragg. I couldn't believe I was back here. I only had five months left to go on my 2-year contract but it seemed like years. I entered the gates and headed to my barracks. I was now attached to the 1/327th parachute regiment. This would be my new home for the next five months.

I headed into the barracks and took a top bunk near the south door. I unpacked and got situated there. I then went to report to the platoon sergeant who happened to be Staff Sergeant Carmichael. I entered his office and said "PFC Nunez reporting for duty." He rose swiftly off his chair and said "I heard you're the Vietnam war hero who's getting the Silver Star. Please have a seat. It's an honor to have you back here." Soldiers would look at my 101st patch on my upper left arm. They knew I wasn't one to mess with.

I started to take this thing a little serious. It had been mentioned in Lederman hospital and maybe before in Japan. I didn't know I was being awarded this medal nor did I really care. I'd give a leg to have my friends back that I lost in Nam'. There were many people in the military especially in this "wartime era" that wanted to go home with a chest full of medals like Audie Murphy. We called these assholes "medal hounds." Those were the idiots who'd get you whacked in the bush. I served my country just like everyone else over there did. I had charged two enemy machine gun nests while under fire trying to get Mendez and an FNG named Wilcox out of harm's way. In the process I was wounded. I knew soldiers who jumped on grenades to save their buddies lives'. Now that was a hero to me. Now I'm here in Bragg and being treated like royalty. I got perks and privileges that NCO's (Non-commissioned officers E-5 and up) couldn't get. I remember a soldier who was on base saluted me as I walked past him one day. I saluted back and laughed my ass off after. These guys here looked at me like I couldn't do no wrong.

I caught wind from a private that we would be going on bivouac for two weeks in a few days. I wanted no part of this BS so I went to sick call and said I had pain in my back. The nurse there at the base hospital gave me some valium and told me to go get some rest. While all these other soldiers prepared for a two-week excursion, I laid in bed listening to music with a hand size radio. I almost burst into laughter as some soldiers wished me well. Hell there wasn't a damn thing wrong with me except I didn't want to play G.I Joe. I'd be perfectly content if they sent me to Vietnam again. But none of this monkey business. In all honestly, I enjoyed the military. I enjoyed the Army. I enjoyed the things I learned and accomplished. Hell I got so used to Vietnam had I made it to my 365 I would have probably re-upped (re-enlisted). My fear had been killed early in my tour and I loved being in the bush with my 60', with my boys. I had seen and gone through too much. My Army career in my mind was finished. Now if they had sent me back to Fort Ord would that have changed my attitude? ABSOLUTELY!!!! But the powers that be wanted to play fuck-fuck games and sent me back across the USA to Fort Bragg. So I gave it back to them. I noticed that there was a small percentage of us at Bragg who were seasoned Vietnam Veterans. You could tell who'd been there and who'd been" in the shit." The others still looked greener than Palmolive soap. There it is!!!!

Once the battalion left for bivouac, I immediately got ready and packed a bag. I went to the small town of Lumberton and rented a motel for the whole week. I'd go into these hole in the wall bars and mingle with the locals. Even some of these restaurants had bars that were jumping. They'd do line dancing and that kind of thing. I remember getting plastered and trying it once with some white girl I met. I ended up falling on my ass. Too much Jack Daniel's that night.

A few nights later I went to this bar called "The Sugar Bar" and met this gorgeous woman named Linda. She was a TEN plus with an amazing body across the board. Hot legs, nice sized breasts, and a face I'll never forget. She told me she was half white half creole. Creole were French mixed with black. I'm telling you she was out of this world. She worked as a registered nurse at a nearby hospital. She told me she was born in Baton Rouge, Louisiana and grew up in Lumberton. Her father was a World War II veteran who fought in the North African campaign against the Germans. He was stationed with the 82nd Airborne Division and became a lifer. They never left North Carolina. This was a blessing to me. I wanted to be with her from the start. Not just sexually but as a relationship. She was smoking hot and I wanted it all for myself. On top of that, she drove an awesome red colored 68' Corvette. Once we left the bar, we went to her place and I rode shotgun. I was pretty lit by then. She had her own house and it was beautifully decorated. I spent the night there having passionate sex with her. I was on cloud nine.

I spent every day at Linda's after that. I never even cared to go back to base because my whole battalion was out in the field. I did go a week later to do my qualifying jump with another battalion to show my face to the higher ups. Also I wanted to keep my jump status which paid me an extra $55 a month. Besides that, I'd go drop off Linda at work and relax at her house. I'd roam around the town and spent a lot of time at the bars shooting billiards. I love billiards. Dad had a table in the garage back home and he'd let us get down to one ball. Then he'd run the table and knock the eight ball in. Our pride would be shattered every time. He'd just play games with us. Nobody could beat Dad. Not in billiards, not in drinking.

I arrived back at Bragg a day before my battalion came back from the field. I got a haircut and shaved. I started hating haircuts and loved my sideburns. I had to get it done though. Once they arrived it was back to barrack life for the day of course. We'd get off around 4pm and then it was off to Lumberton to pick up Linda. She got off around 5pm and I'd wait outside for her. I'd stay with her every night and drive her Corvette to base. The looks I'd get from every soldier from private to colonel was priceless as I drove in every morning. In my head I was on my O.F.P. (own fuckin program). I was having fun now. I was living life to the fullest.

A week later I was told to be in my Class A uniform the next day. Paratroopers wore their Class A greens with our trousers tucked in our boots. Leg units (non-airborne units) couldn't wear them like us. Plus, I had the Screaming Eagle patch on (101st). I'd earned that in Vietnam and that was where my heart was. We were to have a divisional ceremony. It was a big thing. They were decorating our muster area with all kinds of ribbons and whatnot. I was wondering what was so important.

The next day Major General Stevens was on deck. We were all in class A uniforms at parade rest. We all had our maroon berets on (airborne wore maroon berets) and medals if you had some. The next thing I know I hear" PFC Nunez front and center." I couldn't believe it. I went to the front of the entire division and locked at attention. I saluted our commanding officer Colonel Burns. He saluted back with a smile. At that point, I saw Major General Stevens come up to me. I saluted him and he saluted back. He had Staff Sgt. Carmichael next to him who had a small blue box. Major General Stevens then spoke these words: "For your heroic efforts and gallantry in combat in the A Shau Valley in Vietnam on February 13th 1969, I present to you the Silver Star. I also promote you to the rank of Sergeant. It's an honor to have you here Sergeant. I was then pinned by General Stevens and the entire division erupted in a loud "AIRBORNE ALL THE WAY." I couldn't believe it. I had just received the second highest medal in the Army just behind the Medal of Honor. Third highest of all branches behind the Medal of Honor. The Navy Cross and Distinguished Service Cross are in second. It was one of my most prideful memories I had. After that every soldier on base knew who Sergeant Nunez was. You would think my next four months would've been kosher. I was also awarded the Air Medal and Purple Heart. They only got worse.

Since being pinned I was treated like God times ten on base. I was given orders to watch the motor pool which was a no-show job basically. As soon as PT was over, I'd drive back to Linda's and go back to bed. Linda carpooled with a co-worker and let me use the car at my disposal. After a while I started having major flashbacks. I'd find myself patrolling in the Ruong Ruong Valley or the A Shau. I could smell the foliage and the land. It was surreal. I'd shit bricks watching Charlie and a hundred of his buddies charging me. Then I'd see flashes coming from their AK-

47's and I'd wake up hysterical. Perspiration was more like trenched. I mean SOAKED. I couldn't get much sleep anymore and would sleep during the day. I also became more defiant and stopped shaving. I also let my hair grow out.

I went back to base in civilian clothing one day and nobody said a word to me. EXCEPT for Staff Sergeant Carmichael. I could tell he was upset with me. He called me in his office. The door closed behind me. He then laid into me: "Sergeant Nunez, what is going on with you lately? You haven't been showing up to duty and we almost listed you as AWOL (Absent Without Leave) but someone had seen your Corvette in town. You are the highest medal recipient on base and a role model to these younger, greener soldiers. You should act like it. Instead soldiers are looking at you with disgust. You even have a new nickname. They're calling you CRUDBALL NUNEZ!!!! Your hygiene is not up to par by military standards. You haven't had a haircut and you're growing a daggone beard. You can be a goddamn hippie protester in three short months for all I care. I could give a shit. Until then, you will change your ways and act accordingly. Now go home, get a haircut, and shave for pete sakes. Go away Nunez. I expect you looking sharp tomorrow in formation. "

I was so pissed I went to a bar with a few buddies (Johnston and Burgess) who were also Vietnam Vets. I was supposed to get a haircut but I passed. I'd rather go get smashed. We were in this bar when a group of soldiers from the base came in. They were already plastered and were making a ruckus. Then I heard one soldier pass by and utter "These Vietnam Vets think their shit don't stink. I'd eat these three for breakfast myself." I guess he figured nobody was going to test his group or his huge 6'6, 280-pound frame. WRONG!!! My brother Nacho and I had been

112

fighting big dudes since we were small. That didn't scare me. On top of that, if I had any fear I'd left it in the jungles of Vietnam. I tore into that prick and my buddies jumped his group. It was a 10 on 3. We destroyed these idiots and I ended up almost killing the big mouth. The next thing I know is the MP's (military police) came storming in. We all got hooked up and spent the night in the clink. Staff Sgt. Carmichael came to get us out. I didn't want my buddies Johnston and Burgess in trouble. I took full responsibility and was busted down to Private First Class. I didn't even have my rank of Sergeant for a month. Oh well. I didn't give a shit about rank. It didn't faze me. Staff Sgt. Carmichael and Colonel Burns then told me to take a few weeks off. I ended up telling them about my flashbacks and how I didn't want to be there. They wanted my time to end just as much as I did. But I was a decorated war hero. That saved my ass over and over.

The next few months I spent with Linda and rarely on base anymore. As my time was nearing the end, Linda asked me to move in with her. She had really fallen in love with me. But by then, my mind was made up. I was never going to live in North Carolina. I had my family and friends back in California. She just made time pass by easier. I did like her a lot but not enough to stay there. I received better news and was told I could finish the last of my time in California doing "recruiting." I had no plans of doing it but I would be finished with my Army career. It was now September and I heard both my brothers were now in Vietnam. Cirilo was in Chu Lai as a tunnel rat working with the 196th light infantry/26th combat engineers. Nacho was in the 173rd (or "the Herd") Airborne Division in the Central Highlands near Dak To. I couldn't wait to see them once their tours were finished.

In October I told Linda I was going home for recruiting. Once I was finished I told her I'd come back. She was very upset but knew she could not hold me down. Also her life and her career was in North Carolina. I wasn't going to ask her to uproot her life just for me. I just couldn't be tied down nor did I want to be. She had her future and I had mine. She wasn't going to be included in mine though. I gave her my phone number back home and promised to stay in touch. I never did though once I got back home. I resumed life as best as I could. I was still having flashbacks and bouts of anger/depression. Linda called me a month later at Mom's house. Mom answered the call. I told Mom to tell her I went to work in the oilfields in Alaska. She got the hint. That was the last I heard again from Linda. It was a shitty move on my part. My head wasn't right and I had no desire to return there. It was over.

Chapter 14: More Blood Spilled

I was adjusting okay back home in California. I had landed myself a job at Lockheed Aircraft and was making great money. Plus, I was getting a little bit of money from the VA (veterans administration) and college money since I was attending Valley College. Things were looking better for me. I was still in the Army on paper. Other than that, I was free to do as I please. I went to the recruiting duty one time. ONE time I said!!! The first and only time I went it was a joke. Recruiters were in their office playing cards and drinking liquor out of coffee mugs. It wreaked of cigarette smoke and Jack Daniel's. I let them know I was reporting for duty. One of the Sergeants turned and said "if you care to do this fine. If not, don't come back till your discharge papers come in." No need to go there anymore I thought. It brought me back to my high school days when I'd ditch school and go have fun. I was still living with Mom and Dad in Pacoima.

I wrote back to both my brothers (Nacho and Cirilo) in Vietnam. I got a letter back from both separately about a month later. Both were adjusting to Nam' okay and both were still alive. The little fact that most don't know about Vietnam is some soldiers that just arrived in Vietnam wouldn't last a month. They'd either hit a trip wire or Charlie would catch them slippin' on night watch. It was said if you were to get killed in the Nam, it's better to get it within your first week. That way you didn't waste your time and get zapped when you were a "double-digit midget." That meant you had less than a 100 days left in country.

A next few months were me starting to build a business. While at Lockheed I was always thinking about opening my own business like Dad. He had a 9th grade education and started from the bottom. He retired before 50. Not bad for a poor kid with minimal education. I knew I could do it and started looking into some venues to dive into. I really enjoyed construction and pool digging. I could work a tractor like it was nothing. My work ethic was unbeatable and I'd stay hours to finish a project. At Lockheed they'd tell me to go home sometimes because I hated to leave projects unfinished. It was just the way I operated.

I went to visit my biological mother Bertha for the weekend. It was like a semi-family reunion. I saw all of my younger siblings who were still young at the time. Also a lot of my cousins. I also got to see Juanita and Mary. We cooked Mexican food at my mother's house on Boulder Street and sang songs all night. The neighbors probably despised us for keeping the whole street awake. Who cares right? As long as we were having fun. No matter what I stayed close to my direct siblings especially my sisters. All six of us had a strong bond as I mentioned earlier. That has never changed.

Cirilo was with the 196th Light Infantry Brigade (Americal Division). While on patrol in Chu Lai in late 1969, an enemy sniper's round found its mark on him. He was wounded in the upper right arm shattering his bone. He would be medevac'd out and flown home. His time in Vietnam was over for good. He recovered in a VA hospital in El Segundo near LAX airport. It took six months to fully heal.

Nacho had been attached to the 173rd Airborne Division aka "sky soldiers." They are the only unit to ever have an airborne jump in Vietnam (1967). Paratroopers were ineffective as far as a jump was concerned. There were so many damn trees that you would most likely be shredded to pieces on your way down. But these guys at least did it once. His unit was operating in the Central Highlands in Vietnam. Nacho would be attached to a "5-man hog team." These small teams would operate in the jungles with a dog. The dog would go on patrols with them and alert the sky soldiers. Alert them for gooks, booby traps, etc. They proved very effective. They continue to use dogs in wars today like Afghanistan and Iraq. On November 8th 1969 while on patrol, his unit ran into a company of NVA. They engaged in a fierce firefight that lasted an hour. While assisting another sky soldier, an enemy round tore through his left calf and shattered in his left foot. He was also medevac'd out and his leg was saved. Although the round had blown off half his calf, he would still be able to walk with a lot of recovery. He was sent home as well. His time in the Nam' was over as well.

Once Nacho returned to the world, he recovered from his leg wound. The doctors told him he'd never walk again. He beat the odds and fully recovered. He also held many jobs throughout the following years. Ice cream man, RTD bus driver, and a chemical operator at the Chevron oil refinery. He perfected one job better than all these. He became a MASTER SMUGGLER.

Nacho would hire pilots to fly Cessna planes into Mexico and other countries. There they'd load the plane full of grass and cocaine. They would land in the dry lake beds of Palm Springs. Another favorite landing spot was in the Death Valley desert. Every time Nacho disappeared for a week, he'd come back with a grip of CASH. He'd rent RV's and pack up the neighborhood kids. He'd take them camping and cover all the expenses.

On one particular drug run, Nacho's pilot flew too close to the mountains. His pilot misjudged the altitude in the clouds. He clipped the side of a cliff and crashed the plane. His pilot was killed instantly. Nacho ended up with a broken leg. Yet he still managed to save AND deliver the product to its final destination. That guy was incredible!!!!!

The most horrific part was thinking about my mother Bertha. Her three oldest sons went to Vietnam. We all got wounded in the year 1969. I went to visit her after and made sure that she was okay. She said that she knew they both would fully recover. We were cut from a strong cord and nothing was going to stop us from moving forward. It just was not in our will to give up or quit. That was not part of the Nunez vocabulary. It still isn't today.

The holiday season of 1969 went very well. I split my time between Mom and Dad's and my mother's in East L.A. The new year was 1970 and looking very good. My brothers were wounded but they would be coming home soon. They were still recovering in various VA hospitals in California. My brother Mike was still living in Sylmar working at Denny's. He was in love with his sweetheart Mona. He ranted and raved about her all the time. He even spoke about marrying her someday. He told me he was happy that he didn't get drafted. He often would tell us the story about the mail man telling him he'd get his draft orders soon jokingly. Mike didn't pay no mind to it.

Well about a month later I received a call from Mike. He was sort of frantic and was speaking very fast. When I asked him to slow down and speak more clearly he said "I got drafted Kidd.

Can you believe this shit? I have to report to Fort Ord in thirty days." Honestly I really couldn't. All three of us had voluntarily joined the Army. I wasn't sure why he was picked but I guess it was the luck of the draw. Some Americans that got drafted fled to Mexico or Canada. I told Mike I'd go visit him later at the restaurant he worked at. When I walked in I could see him cooking in the back. You could see the life had been sucked out of him. He didn't have any plans whatsoever to go into the military. He was different. But he wasn't going to run away. He was going to answer his country's call and do his service. Little did we know it would end up saving Mike's life.

Chapter 15: MIKE

My brother Mike came out from the back. He sat down and we had coffee. He told me that he wasn't afraid to go into the Army. The only thing that he worried about was leaving Mona back home. Most likely he would have to go to either Vietnam or some parts overseas. Either way two years is quite harsh for some to hold onto. I told him to start getting realistic and just do his term. If it was meant to be she'd be here waiting for him once he had completed his military duty. He didn't like to hear it but he knew I was speaking facts.

Mike started to get his affairs in order before heading out to boot camp. He still worked at the restaurant up until the last week he had left. The rest of the time he spent with his sweetheart Mona and with me. He was bummed out that he was leaving Mona but he wasn't scared to go into the Army. It just threw his life a slight curveball. We all went to see him off at the Ballesteros' house in Sylmar. His friends along with his girlfriend were there. His buddy Jerry and Mona would be driving him off to the airport. He said his goodbyes and we saw them drive away. Mike was about to enter the United States Army that day. On his way to catch a flight to Fort Ord to begin his 8-week boot camp training. Uncle Sam had snatched up the last available Nunez of our family.

It was two weeks after Mike left and I was outside working on my car. Mom called out for me and said there was a taxi out front. I cleaned my hands off and went to investigate. Who was it? It was MIKE!!!! I knew he should've been in boot camp for at least another 6 weeks. What the hell was he doing here? I went to the front gate and there he was with a small bag. He had a devious grin on his face. He was giddy. I found it no laughing matter. Back then if you went AWOL and they caught you, you went to PRISON. Military prisons like Leavenworth to break rocks. I asked Mike what the hell he was doing. He told me he missed Mona and was homesick. He came back to see her for a few days before he went back. I told him he needed to face reality and that the next two years he wouldn't be home. It was a part of life most teenagers don't want to face. It was called growing up. I told him to be ready in a few days so I can take him to the airport. He showed up a week later!!!!

"Alright Kidd I guess you can drop me off at the airport now. I'm going back to Fort Ord." I drove him back to the airport all the while letting him know he had to take the military serious. He was defiant and it was going in one ear out the other. Every sentence I spoke to him was followed with a somber "Yes Jim, Yes Jim. "He just didn't give a shit and was going to do what he wanted. He was going to learn the hard way. He could care less. It's almost like Mike enjoyed pain. I do believe that to some extent. He was going back to face the music.

I called Mike's company commander at Fort Ord and explained the situation and why he left. I felt my brother was naive about certain things in the military and I wanted to smooth things over. I of course mentioned that I was a Vietnam Veteran as were my two older brothers. I explained to him that my brother Mike had some personal issues he had to take care of but now everything was back in order. I gave him my word on this. He said no further action would be done and he would dismiss any write-ups coming to Mike. I thanked him again. After I hung up the phone I felt so relieved. It was a weight off my shoulders. I

went to the backyard and smoked a joint. I couldn't believe
Mike had dodged a bullet. Thank God that was out of the way.

Two and a half weeks had passed without any hiccups. I
received a letter from Mike saying training was going great and
that military life wasn't too bad. I was helping Mom clean up
the kitchen when the phone rang. I dried my hands off and
answered the call. It was Mike. He really sounded happy and
well. I remember getting two calls in boot camp so it didn't
seem out of the norm. I asked him how training was going. He
said he needed another break and was back in Sylmar. He was
hanging out with Mona in a motel next door to the Denny's he
used to work at. I screamed over the phone "WHAT THE HELL IS
WRONG WITH YOU!!! Do you know I smoothed out everything
with your company commander. Now you've gone AWOL
AGAIN!!!! You're so screwed!!!! You're going to get locked up in
the BRIG!!" Mike being his usual self simply replied "Shut up
Jim, I know what I'm doing." I told him to sit tight and I'd be
over there as soon as possible. I was pissed. This was serious
and he wasn't seeing it that way.

I met Mike and Mona at Denny's. I gave him a hug. I told him he
was going to have to go back and soon. Not in a week but
tomorrow. Mona agreed and said she didn't want him to get in
trouble. After Mona left, Mike and I sat at a bar down the
street. We had a few beers and talked. He told me he just
couldn't live without Mona and missed her. I told him there
would be plenty of others wherever he ended up. I think he
seriously got it this time. He knew he couldn't get out of it and
just had to deal with it. I told him I'd drive him myself up there
the next morning. I told him I'd pick him up at the motel at 8am.
The next day I arrived at the motel to pick him up. Mona

answered the door and said he was gone. GONE? What do you mean GONE I asked? She said she'd taken him to the Greyhound bus station at 5am. He took the earliest bus back to Fort Ord. He didn't want to waste any time. She also told me Mike felt bad about leaving boot camp again. He was going to finish with no other monkey stunts. He did just that graduating boot camp and advanced training.

Mike went on to do advanced training right there in Fort Ord. While on liberty on weekends, he stayed in or around the area. He never came back to visit during this time. Instead he would go party or find other women in the towns around Ord. He had become an 81mm Mortar man. Those were the big cylinder looking tubes that you dropped the rockets in and they shot out like a dart from hell. He wrote me saying he was enjoying the training and looking forward to his permanent duty station wherever that would be. He was hoping to stay close to home if possible and dodge Vietnam if he could. After training he got his orders for his permanent duty station. He would be going to Germany. He couldn't believe it. He got two weeks leave after training and spent most of his time with Mona. He must've known by now it would be over once he went to Germany. He'd be 6,000 miles away from home and wouldn't be able to come home on weekends. I gave him a hug and wished him well. He headed to LAX to catch his flight to his new home for the next year: Germany.

Chapter 16: Wedding Bells and a Baby

The year was 1970 and I had a secret I'd held in my pocket for about three years now. I was 20 years old now. I was continuously growing stronger everyday both mentally and physically. This one secret would come to bring me my greatest joys and some of the saddest as well. Around the time I was 17 years old, I had started fooling around with my foster sister Pat. I had been accused one day by her Aunt Emily when we were all playing in the Tujunga wash one day. She was a bitch and I never liked her. She was like a Firestarter. It made me upset and I had the mentality "if I'm going to be accused of it might as well do it." I never thought Pat would do anything to break the rules. She listened to Mom and Dad obediently. I did have a girlfriend at the time named Regina but I didn't care. A lot of times I just thought with my dick and I'm just being real. Anyways we kept it under wraps but then Pat started arguing with me a lot. She wanted more than I did and I didn't see it like that. Once I left to Vietnam I felt relieved. I didn't need no hassles especially since I planned on marrying Regina once I got out of the Army.

When I came back from Bragg the second time I finally ran into Regina. I cussed her out and told her she was dead to me. I told her while I was in Nam' I never received shit from her. She swore up and down that she had written hundreds of letters but got no response. She figured I was done with her. I didn't believe shit coming out of her trap. I told her to go to hell and never to contact me EVER AGAIN.

Now back to Pat. In summer of 1970, we were both working at Lockheed in Burbank off of Hollywood Way. We started messing around more and more. It got tough since we lived in the same house and had to drive far out of town to spend time together. We started going out more. I knew if Dad ever found out he'd hang me by the balls upside down. Mom would probably disown me and want me out of the house. I felt like shit and hating the sneaking around part. I just didn't want to shatter this family. But I was in too deep by this point. Pat was the only virgin left when I started messing with her. She was a plain Jane type who didn't do drugs and rarely drank. She was a good girl. One a parent would be proud of. Unlike me Mr. King of Fuckups lol. We carried on with this charade for the whole summer. Then in late October of 1970 Pat dropped a BOMB on me. She told me she was pregnant!!!!!

I knew right then and there that my life expectancy was very short. Dad for sure was going to kill me. I had no doubt about it. The family that took me in, the love they displayed to me, all the mentoring, was going straight down the toilet. She asked me how I felt and I told her Dad is going to kill me. She was scared just as much as I was. I told her I'd figure something out. Before I left she told me "Jim I'm going to have this baby with or without you." I was scared to death. My head was on a swivel.

I had made up my mind the next day that I was going to be with Pat. I wasn't going to be a worthless father and abandon her. I wasn't going to have my child go through what I went through. I'd be dead before that ever happened. I had accepted my responsibility and was going to be a good father to my child. I was going to be there for them and have a relationship with my kid that I never had with my biological Dad. I was worried that

Pat would open her mouth to her sister Evie since they were close. She laughed at me when I asked her and said "are you kidding me Jim. Of course not." Okay good. We needed to figure out a plan and we needed it soon. I told Pat we'd have to move out together. I was going to be a man and do the right thing. I was going to marry her. She looked amazed when I told her that. She said she was all in and ready to be my wife. We secretly started to look for an apartment and we had to do it fast. Pat was probably 90 pounds soaking wet. Mom and Dad would see her weight gain and know something was up. We both had to get out of that house and move. We relentlessly looked for a place and found one about a week later. We couldn't move in till the second week of November. Geeeez!!! Well at least we had something to shoot for. The two weeks we had to wait were filled with agony and anticipation. But it finally arrived. The day had come to move out of the house: WITHOUT Mom, Dad, Evie, and Grandpa Kinteen spotting us. It was crunch time now. Our hearts were racing. We'd be taking a leap of faith with each other. I was certain my demise was coming soon.

The day came to move out. Dad was driving one of his trucks and would be out all day. Mom had to go meet her friend and do a ton of shopping. Grandpa Kinteen would be at one of his girlfriends' house all day in San Fernando. Evie was going to the beach with her friends in the morning. If we were going to do this right, we'd have to haul ass and get packed. I wanted to be packed up no longer than thirty minutes. I borrowed my buddy Raul's truck which was big. We would have one chance to do this. If we blew it, we were screwed. The only good thing was we had a furnished apartment with brand new furniture. So we wouldn't have to pack beds, dressers, etc.

Believe it or not, we were out of there in less than twenty minutes. As we drove away I remember telling Pat "it's just us now." She nodded with a slight grin and gave me a kiss. We were about to start a family. We both were very excited. We moved in to our new apartment in Sylmar and started unpacking. After we were finished straightening out our things, we packed a bag and loaded up in my car. We were heading to Las Vegas, Nevada to get married. The day was Friday the 13th of November. Go figure.

We got to Las Vegas Friday late evening and booked a room till Monday. We had taken days off work and didn't have to return till Wednesday. Once we got to the hotel, we went to get our marriage license from the courthouse in downtown Las Vegas. We went to a little chapel on Las Vegas Blvd. It was now 130am on Saturday the 14th. We had wedding rings I had previously bought. We exchanged our vows and officially became Mr. and Mrs. Santiago J Nunez. We were married. Our only witness was a housekeeper of the building. So what. I didn't care either did Pat. We were now husband and wife. We'd face the music once we got back home. For now, we'd have a blast here in Vegas and enjoy our time together. No turning back now!!!!

We called a few friends and let them know we were married. Then the inevitable. We'd be calling home. Evie answered the phone and asked where were we. She had seen all of our things gone. So did Mom and Dad. We let her know that we had gotten married. She passed the phone to Mom. She was shocked. She said Dad was outside and he was going to blow a gasket. She was in disbelief and kept repeating "You and PATSY?" She just didn't see it coming. Evie said her and her cousin Norma would fly up to Las Vegas to meet us in a few hours. We said that was fine and would see them up here. We ended up meeting them that afternoon and having a blast the whole weekend. Then came Monday morning. Ughhhhhh man. Not looking forward to this one.

Mike was headed back to the States for some weird reason. He had been in Germany for a year now and was going to finish his time in San Francisco. He called me up and said there were some tests being done on him. He was getting sick over in Germany. They had found something in his lungs but weren't sure what it was. They sent him to the US to undergo further testing. I braced for the worst. I'll get back to this in a bit.

We arrived back at Mom and Dad's house Monday afternoon. Mom was the first to greet us and said congratulations. She was still in shock but what could she do. I think she accepted it for what it is and knew she couldn't change it. She told me she loved us both and was excited about our baby news as well. Mom told me Dad was out back working on the trucks. It was time to man up. I expected to die that day in the backyard.

I went over to find Dad and could see he was underneath one of his trucks. I went next to the truck and said "Hi Dad how are you." I immediately heard silence as his wrench dropped midair out of his hand. My heart sunk to feet. I rolled out quick on his board and rose to his feet. He looked at me with utter disappointment. I started to speak and he put his hand up as to stop me. "I don't want to talk right now. Give me a week and I'll deal with you then." I respected his decision and said ok.

The next week I went over and talked with Dad. He told me he was disappointed but what was done is done. He told me to take care of his daughter and provide like a man should. With that said life was heading in the right direction. We were married and about to have our first child. We had our own place and two cars. We were ready to go all out and make our dreams realities.

On a warm summer Saturday morning our daughter was born. Trina Marie Nunez was born to us on June 19th 1971. Same birthday as my brother Mike. She was born at Kaiser Hospital in Panorama City. We both had tears of joy in our eyes. I actually cried with Pat and was so happy to see a living version of the both of us. It was an amazing and joyous act to witness. Pat was so good during her few hours of labor and I stayed with her the entire time. She was relaxed and didn't look nervous. She said she was but it didn't seem like it. She was such a gorgeous baby and she was ours. I loved holding her and we quickly started to see who she looked like more. It was me of course lol. I had strong jeans I guess. She was the apple of my eye. I was so proud and loved her so much. I would try to be the best father to her. She deserved it. It was the best time of my life.

Chapter 17: Hodgkin's Disease, You S.O.B!!!!!!

MIKE: I had been in Germany (West) for a little over a year now. I was a tanker in the 4th Armored Division. I was living the dream like Elvis who was in the 3rd Armored Division in Germany also back in his days. Once I landed there, I was awestruck. Our base was close to "K-Town" but I went everywhere once I got free time. I really did. I went to Berlin which the wall was still up and divided the country in half. It was an epic sight. Also I went to big cities like Munich and Stuttgart. It was a blast and I was a stranger in a different country. Right up my alley. I was a bona fide loner who didn't need to go out in "crowds." I was having so much fun I started to slowly forget about Mona.

When I got to Germany I wrote Mona a letter and gave her my contact address. I started receiving letters from her professing her loyalty and love to me. I had a slight bit of hope but knew it was a longshot. I had already accepted the facts. Over a period of time I was still writing her. Mind you, I hadn't even slept with another woman yet in the first three months in Germany. As the time past I noticed Mona's letters were dwindling. I started receiving one letter a month instead of 6-7. I knew she had probably met someone knew. Fuckin Jody!!! I came to reality and just let it go for the time being.

Once I knew that shit, I went absolutely BERSERK!!!!! I would go out with my Army buddies for a few beers on Friday afternoons and then disappear into the German nightlife far from our area. My buddies were fun but they liked to get shitfaced drunk and end up with no pussy after getting thrown out by the MP's. That didn't seem like a great plan to me. I wanted to score with some local women who could show me the country and I wasn't going to find it in the bars here. I went exploring.

I started meeting these women on the outskirts of town in little cities probably an hour out from base. To be a little bit more mobile I bought myself a 1969 Volkswagen Beetle. That bug was the shit. I took it on the famous Audobon highway (where there's no speed limit) and drove that thing like a speed racer. I actually blew the engine in four months but I got it replaced for dirt cheap. Anybody who knows about bugs know they're very inexpensive to rebuild or buy parts. I would even load up my bug with my Army buddies and drop them off Fridays in town. They'd ask "Hey Nunez can we go with you?" I'd reply "Sorry guys I work alone." I was fucking like 5 different women spread out through three different cities. It was wonderful and I was treated like a king. We'd go drinking this strong German beer called "Dunkel" out of German steins. Those mugs were daggone mini-kegs. I swear it was a blast.

The "krauts" as we called the Germans were pretty cool dudes. I was actually loving Germany. After a year I wanted to stay there to finish my tour. I didn't care about Mona or anything back home as much to go back to anytime soon. We had our yearly physical and I had 10 months to go on my 2-year assignment. I was planning on staying till my results came back. I walked into the doctor's office and had three male American doctors looking at me with pity. I thought to myself "what's going on here?" One of the doctor's stood up and said "We're sending you to Ramstein Air Base to get a few antidotes and treatment. Then you'll be flying back to the States immediately. Lederman Hospital in San Francisco, California to be exact. "Why am I going back when I have nine months to go. I opted to finish my tour here." The doctor replied "Mr. Nunez.........you have Hodgkin's disease. It's a form of cancer in your lymph nodes." I heard NOTHING after that. My world just shattered like a rock going through a window. I was doomed!!!! I had never heard of Hodgkin's disease before.

How could this be I thought? I started hitting the Bible even more. I always have been religious and stayed pretty consistent with it. Now don't get me wrong I was a sinner beyond a sinner if you catch my drift. But I always had strong faith. It was just a test of fate and it was going to test me till the end. I knew this was going to be an uphill battle but the Lord would be on my side. I was now 19 years old. No way was I going to be cut short. I wasn't going down without a fight. How was I going to tell my family?

Especially my brother Jim. That guy was my hero, my best friend. I loved all my brothers and sisters but Jimmy was my dude. He was the one I always went to for help or guidance. He pulled me out of so many jams. He had "the gift of gab." He saved my ass when I went AWOL twice in boot camp. We fought like brothers and had a blast doing it. Making asses out of ourselves was our forte'. One day I aggravated Jim so bad while he was driving on the 118 freeway. He kept telling me "Not when I'm driving Kidd." I'd reply "You gonna make me? C'mon let's fight sucka." I finally pressed his last button when I back handed him right across the mouth. It was flush. BLAAAAMMMM!!!! Jim immediately pulled his Monte Carlo over on the shoulder. He got out of the car. He went around the passenger door and literally yanked me out the window Dukes of Hazzard style. We begin fighting right there on the shoulder of the 118 freeway.

Some alert and concerned citizens had called the cops on us. Reason I know this is the CHP (California Highway Patrol) rolled up on us two patrol cars deep. Jim had me pinned on the ground and was kicking my ass. He wasn't getting tired either, lol. All of a sudden we hear "FREEZE BOTH OF YOU. GET OFF THAT MAN AND BOTH OF YOU GET UP AGAINST THE WALL NOW." Jim and I started pleading with the cops but they didn't want to hear shit. After they figured out we were brothers and were telling the truth, one of the cops asked "Who the fuck in their right mind would do some monkey shit like this. We had concerned citizens calling in saying a man getting beat to death. What the hell is wrong with you motherfuckers?" Jim said "We're just kids Sir."

I landed in San Francisco in July 1970. I met the doctors who informed me that I was to start treatment immediately. I asked what kind of "treatment." He said CHEMOTHERAPY. I knew what that was and heard stories of what that does to the human body. I was also told my days as a soldier were over. I couldn't believe this. I went outside to a local plaza to use a pay phone. I called Jim and Pat's house. Jim picked up the phone. I told him I was back in the States and would be for the next nine months. He asked why. I told him they had found out in Germany that I had Hodgkin's disease. I was to start chemotherapy in two days. The phone went silent.

JIM: I received a call from my brother Mike in July of 1970. He told me had a form of cancer called Hodgkin's disease in his lymph nodes. He told me I was going to start chemotherapy in two days. The phone slid out of my hand. I dropped to the floor. Pat came to see what was wrong and I just cried against the wall. She picked up the phone and talked to Mike. She had a conversation with him for a while. I went outside and lit up a cigarette. I wanted to escape my worst fears. I couldn't lose Mike. We were like twins. That close. Even throughout our foster homes and whatnot we always were tight. He was my roadie my sidekick. We'd kick each other's ass just out of GP. It was just the way we were. There was no way I could see life without him. I got on my knees and prayed to God to make my brother better. Although he took longer than expected God would eventually answer my prayer. One thing I've learned in life is that God answers prayers when the time is right, not just when we need him for a favor!!!!! I had faith he'd bring him out of this. I would be right about it too!!!! Praise the Lord!!!!!

MIKE: You know we often get lost in our own world. We mark down things on our calendars that we have plans for. Or things we intent to do. Go on a trip, meet a fitness goal, but never do we mark down our own death date. People who are naïve will say things like "if I was a millionaire everything would be okay." Most people in this world think like that. That you can buy your way out of something or money can buy remedies for your problems. Well maybe for a few. But NOBODY can buy time. That is what we all want more of and it seems to go faster as each day passes. Nobody's immortal. Money, jewelry, and credit cards are worthless in Heaven. God's love and eternal life is thee ultimate goal for those whose souls are not blackened with darkness. Regardless of my situation, I was ready for war. Hodgkin's was my mortal enemy. I had God and my family on my side. I was determined to beat this shit!!!!!

Chapter 18: Life's Blessings n Horrors

Mike was on medications and he came to live with us. He still had Hodgkin's but it was being contained so far. His Army career was over and he received a medical discharge. Pat and I invited Mike to move in with us. We loved having him there at the house. He loved taking care of our daughter Trina and would play with her every waking second. He loved being an uncle to her. Mike and I would play rough with her and even though she was small. I knew she would be a fighter like her Daddy. I was one proud Dad. Pat loved being a Mother as well. Pat didn't know much about raising children etc. I had experience raising and taking care of my younger siblings that came along. I showed her how to change a diaper, get a bottle ready, and take care of our daughter. She was very receptive and wanted to learn more and more. As I think back, she learned pretty quick.

There was something that wasn't completely right though. Still going through nightmares, still feeling depressed. I had guilty feelings about being alive while my friends died in Nam.' I couldn't understand how and why I survived. It was eating me alive. Another thing that wasn't going great was our marriage. I had found out why my I hadn't ever heard from my ex-girlfriend in Vietnam. Pat played a part into sabotaging that. I felt backstabbed and betrayed by the one person I thought wouldn't do that to me. It left a sour taste in my mouth. I tried to write it off saying to myself I'm already here might as well move forward and not it in the past. I later found out that I couldn't.

I still had the killer instinct on. One thing people who have never seen combat is you just don't shut that off like a light switch. It just doesn't turn off that easily. I had a cache of weapons in the house and a couple of bowie knives. My two rifles (a 30-06 Remington) and a (CAR-15) were my favorites. I'd go rabbit hunting in the mountains just to kill. I'm just being honest. I know it sounds fucked up but better than humans right? Hunting these little bastards was work. They were smart. I always found a way of flushing them out. I even took Pat one time. She wanted no part of it so I never took here again.

One day, Mike had taken off for the day. He had some VA appointments in West L.A. Instead of spending the day happy together, we ended up in a fuckin argument. I can't even tell you what it was about nor do I remember anything that happened in those two minutes till I heard Pat weeping and calling out my name "JIM." I found myself with my Remington 30-06 with the muzzle two inches away from her head. Our daughter was in the other room sleeping. I'd racked a round in the chamber.

PAT: Jim and I really had some rocky times during our years of marriage. I can't remember but it was rough times dealing with him. I didn't know what was going on with him and he never talked to me. So this particular day we had gotten into an argument and I went to the room crying. I was on my knees at the edge of the bed. The next thing you know I hear Jim come in the room. I didn't look up as my hands covered my face. What got my attention quick is when I heard a round slam in the chamber of his rifle. I knew that sound from when I went hunting with Jim. I looked up and the muzzle was almost against my head. "OH SHIT I'm screwed, "I thought to myself. I stopped

141

crying and immediately thought of my daughter Trina who was in the other room. I wasn't scared anymore but heartbroken. I remember thinking to myself "Damn I only made it to 22!!!! My daughter's going to be without a Mom." I was crushed. That thought knocked the fear out of me. Jim was pointing the rifle at my head and speaking in Vietnamese which I couldn't understand. His eyes were black and he was not here. His mind was back in the war. I spoke up and said "JIM WHAT ARE YOU DOING? JIM!!!!!" He then snapped out of it and looked confused. He broke into his gun cabinet and grabbed all his weapons. He went to the front yard and I heard him open the garage. I had just cheated death at 22. Damn that was close.

JIM: I snapped out of it and saw myself pointing my rifle at Pat's cranium. What the hell? How did I get here? I went to my gun shed and grabbed my rifles, shotgun, and four handguns. I popped open the garage and got the biggest sledgehammer I could find. I emptied the 30-06 as it was loaded and started breaking the weapons to pieces. I was so ashamed of myself and scared too. I never wanted a firearm in my house EVER again!!!!! I spent an hour tearing up all my weapons in my front yard. That was it. I wouldn't be in that situation ever again. Scared me to death. Pat told me I should go to the VA and get checked out. I agreed and told her I was sorry for everything. You would think she would have resented me but her first words out of her mouth were "I love you Jim." She was an incredible woman and I have the utmost respect for her till this day. In the years we were married I never "wanted." My lunches would be made, my work clothes ironed, the baby fed and clean, house clean, the works. She NEVER once called me a curse word or anything close. She had her faults but the mass majority was mine. I have never ducked from that. I have no excuses nor care to create one. My mind was just so screwed and I had nowhere to turn. I was lost man. COMPLETELY.

There was a bundle of good news that came in January 1973. I had just gotten off of work at Lockheed and picked up my daughter who was waiting for me at the door. I gave Pat a kiss and walked in the house with my daughter in my arms. Pat asked me and Mike to come to the kitchen for dinner. We all sat at the table and I put Trina in her high chair. Pat then got quiet and had a big smile on her face. "Jim I'm a month and a half pregnant." I jumped out of my chair and went to hug her. She was excited and Mike got up to hug her also. I was on cloud nine. This was great news. We had a growing family. She was due end of August middle of September. Somewhere around that period. About three months later we learned that she was having a boy. Oh man, I'm going to have a son!!! I told Mike about it and he was just as thrilled. Mike loved playing with Trina and my son would be close to him too. Mike asked Pat and I what we were going to name him. I said Jimmy and Pat said James Robert. Either way he would be a Jimmy Jr. Just like his Daddy.

It wasn't all peaches and cream though. Our marriage started to hit a snag. I started going out a little too much. Then I started cheated on Pat. She knew it I could tell. Women have this intuition and sense about things. I wasn't sabotaging our marriage but I just had a bad taste in my mouth about the whole Regina incident. But I had no excuses in the long run. It was just the way I was feeling at the time right or wrong. There were DAYS that went by where we wouldn't speak a word to each other. Pat had quit her job at Lockheed when Trina was born and was a full time homemaker. I just took for granted a lot of things. I was down but not out. I never quit. In anything I ever did. I went to check into the VA for help. I ended up going berserk and was put in the psych ward for six months. They wouldn't release me. Ain't that a bitch!!!!

On August 29th 1973, James Robert Nunez was born at Granada Hills hospital. There was only one problem. I wasn't there. Mom, Dad, Mike, Evie, and her husband Juan showed up. I was still in the psych ward at the Sepulveda VA. I couldn't get them to release me so I tore more shit up. The anger just kept building and building. When I finally was released I was driven home by Mike. Once I got in the house I went straight to see my newborn son. Pat gave me a hug and Trina as always jumped in my arms. I felt like I was in prison for years and just released from custody. We now had two kids and I was fine with that. We tried to be as loving as a family could. Sometimes it worked, sometimes it crashed hard!!!! That's life though. Sometimes you get blessed and sometimes you get horrified. Due to our sinful nature, it's always been a battle between good versus evil.

Chapter 19: Balancing Act

Juggling life can sometimes be a balancing act. You try to stay even keel on everything that's going on in life. Sometimes it works and sometimes it doesn't. You just try to do the best you can. That's exactly what I was doing and trying my hardest. With two kids and a wife, things can get difficult sometimes. But if you work as a team it really helps out.

Pat and I had a good system going. Having Mike there at the house was a blessing also. He would always ask us if he could take Trina and Jimmy to McDonald's. They had these big playpens for kids and Mike would spend hours there with them. He enjoyed every minute of it. Pat and I would either stay at home and enjoy each other's company, go out to a movie, or to Mom and Dad's house. Her sister Evie and husband Juan had a newborn baby girl Lisa Marie. She was born in January of 1973. One day we went over there to visit and shoot billiards with Dad. Juan and I got this brilliant idea. We challenged Dad to a drinking fest. He chuckled to himself, shook his head, and looked at us dead in the eyes. "Are you sure you want to do that?" We both said yes and he smirked. "Good luck" he said as he broke the rack of balls.

The next thing you know we are not only losing every game of billiards but also getting shitfaced. Dad could drink and nothing would faze him. He wouldn't say anything except for "you okay there" with the biggest smirk you could imagine. We were getting hammered and Dad just kept kicking our butts. We were backed up with shots of tequila and he would make a comment like "you know you both are two behind." We couldn't catch up nor win a game. Juan and I were inside Mom's garden about a half hour later. We were under the avocado trees throwing up our lungs. I could see Dad laughing in the background. He peeked through the kitchen window and said to the girls "hey girls I think your husbands are sick out here." Pat, Evie, and Mom come outside to see what's going on. They started laughing too as Juan and I were crawling through the plants. I fought Dad and Dad won!!!!

Pat and I started to do other things that most families do. We started going to the lakes a lot. We'd fish off these rented pontoon boats in Castaic, Pyramid, and Lake Piru. We would get to the lake early in a rented motorhome and get our gear out. Pat would pack up the picnic basket with all kinds of food, snacks, and drinks. It was awesome. Then I'd get the boat rented and we'd all climb aboard. We bought the kids little fishing poles and would set them up for them. I'd drive slow so we could troll along the edges of the lake. It was great. Once we anchored we'd eat lunch and take a dip in the lake. We all jumped in and come out. Sunbathing as a family on the aft of the boat. It was fun to see my family happy. I was really trying to make this marriage work.

I had a great job working at this manufacturing company called Pioneer Flinko. It was located in South Gate. It was a company that made paper products and textile. I was a mechanic there and making killer dough. This is when Dad's teachings on the trucks and cars came into play. I had learned mechanics from Dad. He would teach me how to break down a car or truck all the way down to the shell and back. I had weekends off and we had plenty of money to play with. Pat took care of the house so it was perfect.

We took this one trip I will never forget. We rented this awesome motorhome state of the art. I drove the family all the way up to Shasta Lake in Northern California. It was a 13-hour drive in the motorhome but the views were amazing. We rode the coastline once we pasted the Bay Area. We'd also stop off at sightseeing spots and take pictures together. It was July and the temperatures were a crisp 80 degrees with a gentle breeze. Clean air since you're up 8,000 plus elevation.

We did three days at Shasta Lake and rented a boat all three days. It was great and we caught fish which Pat cooked for us. We had our own bed and the kids had roomy sleeping quarters in the motorhome. I loved it when the kids caught this small fish the last day. Trina wanted to grab the damn fish before I could take the hook out. Jimmy just watched from a distance. He never said much. Trina was his mouthpiece. Pat and I used to observe them and laugh. Trina was definitely the one who liked to explore.

The next lake on our list was Goose Lake an hour north of Shasta Lake. This lake was smack in the middle of the Oregon-California border. We fished off the river banks and took long walks. We'd leave our campsite to explore. Fishing poles, picnic basket, and drinks is all we needed. By now the kids were both four and two respectively. We watched as some fisherman caught their trout. I remember Trina running up to the man and asking if she could take out the hook. The man said "of course just watch your fingers." Yup that was Daddy's girl. We retired after three beautiful days camping in Goose Lake. It was time to go home.

Things between Pat and I were a roller coaster. We were having issues and she didn't trust me at the time. I didn't blame her but damn I wasn't going to be crucified for the rest of my life. We saw a marriage counselor at the VA but it did us no good. We just tried our best. Pat started hinting to me that she wanted one more kid. I was happy the way our family was and didn't really think we needed another one. I told her she should get her tubes tied. That way we would be more focused on our family that we had. She said she'd think about it.

Around 1975 our marriage was on life support about to flatline. Pat and I rarely spoke and there was animosity on both sides. We kept our cool in front of the children. Behind our bedroom door was stacked with tons of arguments. If our door had a voice it would be screaming for days. I just didn't want to be away from my kids. They were my world. I didn't want to fail them. Tensions were high. Our house of love had turned into a house of pain.

Mom invited us to an event held by Kathyrn Kuhlman. She was a born again Christian and TV evangelist. She was very popular and some had even witnessed miracles. I invited my brother Mike who was worsening from all the chemo treatments. Doctors were thinking he'd only have "months" left if it didn't go away. As we sat there in the arena listening to Kuhlman speak, I broke down. I prayed hard and started balling uncontrollably. I wanted Mike to be healed and my marriage work. One was answered that day.

As I was on my knees praying I looked over at Mike. He suddenly had an illuminating glow around his whole body. I was frozen in place. I felt the love of God. It spread throughout my body and the most loving feeling passed through me. There was Mike praying to God and I was witnessing a miracle. Nobody else could see this but me? How could this be? I felt a peace and knew Mike would be okay from here on. I balled in joy and went over to Mike. I told him," Kidd you are healed. Don't be surprised when you go back to the doctors and they tell you your cancer is gone." Mike had felt the healing apparently. He kept saying "I'm healed Jim, the Lord has healed me." A few days later Mike had a doctor's appointment. His doctors were STUNNED!!!!!

The doctors told Mike he couldn't find anything in his lymph nodes and must do more tests. They finally came back and told Mike it was unexplainable. The medical term they used for miracles was "spontaneous remissions." He was cancer free!!!!!! He came home and told us the news. We hugged and cried together. We knew where this came from. Straight from Heaven above. God didn't let us down. Nor did we think he would. The power of prayer and faith is undisputed. With a month, Mike and I were back to our antics. Slapping the life out of each other and fooling around. Kidds!!!!!

Christmas of 75' was one to remember. We got the kids a bunch of presents and I bought Pat a nice necklace. Mike and I set up the tree that year. Also our lights on our house were unbeatable. We got a big Frosty the Snowman outside our front yard. It lit up every night and people on the block would ask where I got it from. I said a friend gave it to me. Those things back then weren't ready available for sale. I had actually bartered for it from a friend who used it onset at the studios in Burbank. He was a grip who built fake backdrops, stages, etc.

The kids went ballistic when we lit it up the first night in December.

I also bought Jimmy this humungous race track with the cars attached to it. The race cars were remotely operated and he was happy when he saw it built. It was ready for him to play and we raced a few times. The cars stayed on track and were lightning fast. If you went too fast the car would fly off the track. Then Mike says to Jimmy, "let your Uncle Mike give it a try." After he got the remote from Jimmy he leaned over and said to me "I'll bet you a dollar I'll kick your ass on this." My response "it's a bet." We were off to the races. Jimmy never got to touch his track again. After two hours of making those cars go crazy and many dollars traded, we blew the cars out COMPLETELY. All of a sudden the fun was gone. I felt bad. We went berserk like little kids. We never had things like this growing up so we were experiencing things first hand like the kids were. We were so competitive and it always turned into a wager. Now I couldn't just run to Gemco or Fedco to buy Jimmy a new track. Hell it was Christmas morning!!! Everything was closed. I told Jimmy the track didn't work properly and I would pick him up one better than this broken one. At 2 years old he wasn't no fool. But he just shook his head and humbly said "Ok Daddy." I bought him a new one the next day. Mike and I never touched it either, lol.

Mike moved out the following year and moved to San Fernando off Maclay Street. He had gone to beauty college to learn to be a hairdresser. I knew what he was up to. He wanted to go into that field so he could "hunt" if you catch my drift. I picked him up from school one day in North Hollywood to see what he was doing. I saw three brunettes come out the door. All "TENS" to the max. I mean "CANNED HEAT." I told him I'd be picking him up again soon. He then told me "Jim this is my realm. I don't want you sniffing around my area. You understand me. "I told him to go screw himself. We both busted up laughing.

It was June of 1976 when Pat and I were at the dinner table. Things were still rocky due to my infidelity and time lapses away at night. We were having an amicable conversation over a homemade spaghetti dinner. She said "Jim I'm two months pregnant by the way. I'm keeping it too so don't even ask. My mind is made up." How this couldn't be I thought. I'd had a vasectomy a year earlier. This couldn't have happened. I told Pat she was mistaken. There's no way since I had a vasectomy. I told Pat she was the one who told me to get one in the first place. I wasn't falling for this one. Then I looked at her and knew she wasn't kidding. She said "I guess it didn't work." Yeah no shit Captain Obvious!!!!! I knew Pat would never cheat on me so I knew this was all me. I thought to myself, we're barely making it work and now another baby on the way. I wasn't too happy about it but it was Pat's choice. I guess one of my swimmers were defiant. Turns out, it would be a blessing in disguise.

On Thursday January 20th 1977 my second son Adrian Miguel Nunez was born in Granada Hills hospital. He looked just like me. All of my kids did but he looked like me the most. I was happy Pat had stuck to her guns on this one. I had three kids now and I was trying to make our marriage work. The flashbacks were unforgiving and the VA was no help at all. They treated murderers on death row better than veterans were treated at the VA. I hated that place. I was going to go to battle against the VA. First though I had a fight I had to take care of at my workplace. It would be yet another test of faith.

Chapter 20: Don't Call Me Sir!!!! I Work for a Living

RUBEN: My name is Ruben Spring. I was born on July 16th, 1953, years after the Nunez siblings. I was born in General Hospital in East Los Angeles, CA. I had never met my father and rarely my mother Bertha. By the time I was three years old, I was a resident at McLaren Hall. I was moved to the Ballesteros home. The parents were Frank and Lucy. Wow, let me tell you about them.

I went to their home along with brothers Mike and Cirilo. It was a nice home in Sylmar, CA. They had a lot of space and were very warm people. Frank started teaching me things I never knew about. He was the first father figure in my life. I took to him and Lucy like no other. Very loving.

After about 7 months of living here, Lucy needed to go back to school. Frank advised the three of us about the situation. They wouldn't be able to properly care for us anymore. WONDERFUL I thought. Now where were we going to live? They told us that Frank's parents who lived three houses down would take us in.

We would move to Gramps and Grammas as we called them. We would not be far from Frank and Lucy. Now we were under their household. It is also where my hell on earth would begin. It wouldn't come from Gramps though. The one who tormented me like no other would be Grammas.

It was very peculiar that she started whopping my ass on a daily basis. Now she would ONLY do this when Gramps went to work. As soon as he was out of the house, she'd come looking for me. I mean, her demeanor would change like a light switch had been flipped. I'd haul ass and dive head first underneath the bed for cover. She'd crawl and yank me out for a longer beating. When she was finished, she was breathing like a boxer who'd just finished the 12th round. Sweat dripping and breathing hard.

Like always, once Gramps arrived, things were normal. She would send me to my room without dinner sometimes. The whole thing that screwed my mind up was this: AFTER my ass beatings, she'd come late at night with a bowl of food crying. I'm talking the uncontrollable crying you see in the movies. Then she'd utter the words, "I Love You."

It messed me up in my mind. How does one person beat a small child like a grown person? Then to turn around and tell you I love you. I could never understand that nor can I to this day. She honestly had mental issues in my opinion.

Gramps would teach Mike and I how to ride horses. He eventually got us into pro bull riding. Back then, Western movies were BIG. Mike and I loved those shows. We'd dress like cowboys too. Gramps would take Mike and I traveling to many competitions. We'd attend bull riding competitions in Montana, Idaho, Nevada, Oregon, etc. It was a great time and Gramps would be there for us.

Once when I was around 15 years old, Gramps took off for his morning errands. Like clockwork, Grammas comes in and takes a swing at me. I caught her hand and told her "NO MORE." She was in awe and tried to wrestle her hand away. I had her hands pinned against her and repeated "NO MORE." I left the room and walked to Frank and Lucy's house. I knew she'd be worried about me ratting her out. What really blew my mind years later was this one fact: I told Frank about how horrible his Mom treated me. He told me that he was never abused ever. Neither were his siblings. That didn't make sense. Maybe she just hated me period!!!! Even through all that I still showed her love. Kids are stupid sometimes, lol.

I excelled in high school and joined the cross country team. I went to Sylmar High School. Home of the Spartans. I took a lot of pride in the sport and earned a letterman. I could run like Forrest Gump. I had stamina and conditioning was the key.

Mike and I both got jobs at the local Denny's restaurant during high school. We both were cooks and busboys. I loved working there and loved their food too. We'd make sky high plates and take them home. We also got a chance to meet a lot of people. Later in my early 30's, Denny's would send me to Australia to open up a restaurant there. I was there for 30 days and it was a beautiful country. 15-hour flight STRAIGHT through. When I got back to Los Angeles, I had major jet lag. I loved to seek new adventures.

I ended up joining the US Army about a year after high school. I served two years and got to visit many countries. It was a great thing and I would gladly do it again. All my older brothers had

156

joined the Army. I knew I had to serve my country also. I believe everyone should join at least for two years.

Around 21 years old, my brother Jimmy had invited me to LA. There was going to be a gathering at my brother Nacho's house. I really didn't want to go because I knew my Mother Bertha would be there. In my opinion, she never really gave a damn about me. She never went to visit me while I was in foster care.

Jimmy convinced me to go and I finally agreed. As soon as I came to the porch, my Mother Bertha gave me a cold stare. She went inside and into her room. My sister Juanita tried to get her to come out but to no avail. I was completely shunned by her but it didn't matter to me. The way I coped with not having my real mother around was simple.

I told myself she had died at eight years old. It helped me cope with reality and not to believe in pipedreams. That just made things worse when you indulged in a world of BS. I will say this though; it was great being around my family.

I lost contact with all my family from 1980-2012. In that time, I suffered a lot especially around the holidays. It hurt not having family around. It could be lonely at times but I trucked through it all. I didn't feel sorry for myself and did the best I could. Sometimes I'd be rich and sometimes I'd be homeless. But I made it through it all.

I got into kickboxing and then started training boxers. I always loved the sport of boxing. It took a lot of discipline and heart to achieve it. Not everyone can become a world champion. I teamed up with a great friend of mine who was also a trainer. His name is Deanie Crisp. A man I respect highly. One day I go see Deanie and tell him I've found the next world champion. His name was Johnny Avila. I gave him his nickname. "The Electrifying" Johnny Avila. He was a tough street kid from Palmdale, CA.

Out of all the fighters I've trained, Johnny Avila had the most heart. He was a gentle, humble guy. He fought his ass off when he fought Oscar De La Hoya. He dropped him in the FIRST round with a stiff jab. They called it a slip but we knew what happened. Even though the fight was stopped in the 9th round due to a cut on Johnny, I knew he did well. His conditioning was superb. He'd eventually become Lightweight Champion of the world (IBO).

Boxing would take me on the road four months at a time. I'd go back to Palmdale for a week to rest. Then I'd be back on the road to train fighters in states like Idaho, Nevada, etc. It was draining but a wonderful experience. I still train young fighters here and there today. I love talking to troubled youths who went through issues I had. I will continue that till the day I die.

The only MAJOR regret I have in life was being away from my one and only child Kevin for years. His mother was the love of my life. The only one I ever had to be exact. Going into the service split us apart. When I returned, I got to see my son. A month later, I learned Kevin and his mother had moved. They resided in Pennsylvania. They still do till this day.

I recently became in contact with my son around 2014. I just wanted to tell him that I was sorry for not being there for him. I didn't want him going through life not knowing his father like I did. But I didn't want to disrupt his life. He has been very receptive to me and I admire him so much for that. I love him and have never stopped loving him. His mother has done an awesome job raising Kevin. I have nothing bad to say about her nor will I ever.

I reunited with my family in 2012. I had never met any of my younger brothers and sisters. My youngest brother David had a party at his house. It was nice meeting the young siblings. Our family has been big since the beginning. I love how our nieces and nephews greet me. They all have manners and are very loving. My brothers and sisters did a good job raising their kids.

Now, 2016, I am 63 years old. I continue to work for the Seeber family business: Seebers Excavation. They are a family who I love dearly. I work as a concrete finisher. I'd been taught that trade years ago by Frank and Gramps. Still enjoying time with my family. I've lost three brothers since I've reunited with the whole family. I'm glad I got to spend time with them before they passed. Life's too short for BS and bickering. Everyone is entitled to their own opinion. Whether political or personal, we should respect each other. What's real is real though.

Chapter 21: My Religious War

I had been excelling at my job and learning new roles. They wanted me to take a position as the head mechanic. It was occupied at the time by a man named Edward. He had 30 years in and was planning to retire soon. There were five others who had more time in than I did. But I knew if I went for it I would get it. The boss loved my work ethic. He loved my passion to learn. I craved for more knowledge. It was just the person I was.

Once Edward retired we all put in for the position. It would take a few weeks to find out who got the job. I honestly forgot about it. Then came the time when they'd let us know. I walked to my boss's office. He kicked up his feet on the desk. He lit up a cigarette and tossed me one. He asked how I liked working here at Pioneer Flinko. I told him I enjoyed the job and the others mechanics. We all helped each other out. We had a great espirit de corps there. There was no backstabbing within us. "Well, Jim you got the position. Congratulations and don't blow it." I shook his hand and walked out the door smiling. My co-workers were happy for me and knew I'd be the one selected.

I had been attending the Seventh Day Adventist church in Sylmar. The holy day for us was the Sabbath which fell on Saturdays. I asked my boss if I could have Saturdays off due to religious obligations. He said not a problem and complied. I loved it and it gave me relief to go to church. I was really trying to fly straight and mend things with Pat. I had stopped fooling around on the side and stopped smoking marijuana. I wanted to do right.

Saturdays were fun for us as a family. Pat would get the kids ready and I'd pack up the car with our bags. Also Pat would cook dishes the night before for our Sabbath potluck. Now our potluck was like a feast from Heaven. It really was. Everybody that attended church would bring dishes of different foods. Since our church had every race in the book, it was like a world buffet. We would put the trays in ovens in our faculty room to reheat once services ended. In fifteen minutes, all these trays were ready. We would have one big prayer and then hit the food. The children and families mingled all into one. It was beautiful and it was a day-long celebration. Around 6pm we'd pack the empty dishes and kids in the car. I was really moving in the right direction.

Pat and I started to get closer believe it or not. It was short lived. Then one thing that started to come up in arguments was money. We would give tithes to the church and she started to resent that. We had enough but Pat was tight at times. I wasn't. I mean I could see her point but there were more important things than ones on this earth. It aggravated me that she didn't share my visions and beliefs. I told her I'd continue to attend church with or without her. She was Catholic and could go to her church on Sundays for all I cared.

I had secured these days at work. For eight long months they had accommodated me for my church obligations. I got so into the church I started teaching bible studies on Wednesday nights. I would go straight from work to the church. I'd be there till 9pm at night. I'd come home and play with the kids for a bit. Once again, Pat and I were silent towards each other. I really needed support but instead got crap in my hand. I tried to block it out and be loving to her anyways. That only worked for a while.

My boss came to me and told me our relief mechanic had quit. Since he was covering for me on Saturdays they had nobody left. I told them to open up a bid for a relief. That would solve the problem right then and there. The boss said that he couldn't do that since nobody was qualified. Now this really is the point when I became unraveled.

I told the boss that there was plenty and I was NOT going to work on Saturdays. It was no problem for eight months and we had mechanics to cover. I believed this was a pure test of faith. I was not going to buckle under any pressure. If I was going to lose my job in the process, I knew I'd win it back. I had the utmost faith in God. I would be put to the test.

The next Saturday came and we were getting ready for church. I had gotten up early and started pressing my suit. Pat asked if I was going to work. I replied" ABSOLUTELY NOT." She shook her head and went to get the kids ready. The phone rang and I picked up. It was my boss. He asked if I was coming to work. I told him no. He knew I wasn't. He explained to me the severity of the situation. I told him I did. He replied "I don't want to lose you Jim but I've got a business to run." I told him "do what you gotta do" and hung up. I didn't have time to hear complaining. Plus, this wasn't going to ruin my Sabbath day.

I went back to work Monday morning. There's my boss Bruce waiting for me. Let's talk Jim he said to me. We walked in his office and he asked if I was coming in on Saturday. I said no. He said he'd have to let me go. I told him I had rights and I'd have the EEOC (equal employment opportunity commission) on him. I told him to choose wisely since I knew I'd win my job back. He handed me my check and wished me luck. I told him I'd be back.

I went to the EEOC in downtown Los Angeles and filed a claim. They said I was unjustly let go and we'd have no problem securing my job back. It was a joyous feeling knowing I'd beaten these guys. I'd been there seven years and never had a problem. Now all of a sudden they wanted to play games. They would be paying me out in the end.

While I was filing my claim I hooked up a better paying job. His was working for Clark forklifts. I was going to receive more pay and no problems having my Saturdays off. PERFECT!!!! God working his magic. It was in Northridge which was only ten minutes away from the house. No more freeways to work. Local now baby!!! I worked Monday through Friday from 7am-3pm. I even got an hour lunch, PAID. I couldn't have asked for anything better.

About four weeks later I was summoned by the EEOC to downtown L.A. I was told I was awarded my job back. I also would receive a check in two days for $2,800 dollars. I would also receive a check for all the back pay I was owed. Blessings, blessings, and more blessings. I loved it. I would be able to go back to work anytime. I had no plans to return to my old job. But I was going to show them something.

I took the next day off from Clark which was a Friday. I walked into Pioneer Flinko wearing my Clark forklift shirt. I walked in and I could see all the mechanics' jaws drop. I loved seeing it. I was greeted by Bruce who stuck his hand out. He said "welcome back Jim." I laughed at him. I simply came here to turn my work badge in saying "I QUIT." I had no intensions of returning. I went there to teach Bruce and management a lesson. They should read the labor laws more extensively. I told him he could mail my check to me. I walked out of that place with pride. I had said goodbye to my friends there. I was already going in a different direction.

One thing I felt was vindicated. I felt this wonderful feeling inside. I was able to witness first hand God's blessings. His work had been done with ease. While everyone doubted him, I never did. It made me feel humble. It also displayed that the Lord was always there by my side. Through it all he never leaves our side. If anyone leaves anyone, it's us that commits that sin. He will never forsake us. He makes miracles happen.

Things went on as planned for a while. I quickly received a promotion and was working in the mechanic shed now. Clark was a fast growing company and they started opening up other shops. I would go help these startups throughout the valley and beyond. I would set up the mechanic shed and order all necessary parts. Then I'd order all tools. They were delivered fast and we'd set up. Then I'd show the mechanic at the new shop how to operate. It was a blast. I was getting paid to teach others. I was only at my shop in Northridge on Mondays and Fridays. The rest of the time I was working at other locations.

Chapter 22: Our War Back Home

The problems that followed myself and many Vietnam veterans were these three pains: The VA, PTSD, and Agent Orange. I will discuss each in detail so forgive me if I go too fast. The VA was only paying me 30% rated. This was meager pay and I was fighting these morons since I came back. They had yet to admit they had used to the chemical in Vietnam called Agent Orange. They also didn't acknowledge PTSD had affected veterans coming back from the war. These people were ruthless I swear. Here's one of their favorite forms of dealing with veterans. They'd issue us a bag full of different drugs and send us on our way. In the process that you happened to take all these pills, you'd be so blown out of your mind. Then you'd forget to push your VA claim for more money. It was blue-printed by these idiots. They knew exactly what they were doing. It worked a lot too. There are tons of veterans that became worn out and gave up. They got tired of the closed doors, the unwanted feeling, and the drugs. Sadly, many died due to suicides including gunshot wounds, needles in their veins, or overdoses. The VA didn't give a damn. One veteran gone meant one less problem to deal with. One less potential check to write. I couldn't stand them and vowed to deliver the crushing blow to the VA.

PTSD had been taken us over. Nacho and I were suffering bad. We just didn't want to admit it. I'll give you a prime example on how warped our minds were. Nacho and I each had a cache of weapons. My cousin Huero had a few of his own too. We'd go hunting together usually in the Corona mountains. This was before all the housing was built. Back then it was a deserted wasteland. The mountains resembled Vietnam's jungles a little bit.

Nacho and I would walk parallel on separate sides of the valley mountain. Huero would walk below on the valley floor. We'd be hunting. Anything that moved we blew to pieces. We still had that killer instinct. It doesn't shut off just by a snap of a finger. After seeing no rabbits or movement of any sorts, Nacho and I became impatient. The next thing I see is a round crack about ten feet in front of Huero. I looked to my left and saw Nacho keying in on Huero. He was laughing as he fired the second burst. I joined in simultaneously. The next thing we see is Huero running away cursing and screaming.

While I kept firing near Huero, I heard the "CRACK" five feet to my left. The round impacted and shattered the hard dirt. I saw Nacho was aiming on me now. I yelled out "Oh ok you wanna play like that Kidd? Take this." I fired near Nacho's position. He immediately high-tailed it behind a large granite boulder. Once he was behind it I told him to stay down. He yelled back "Ok I'm ready Kidd." Once I heard that, I laid down a magazine from my CAR-15. Right at his position. Once that was empty, I picked up my 12-gauge shotgun and emptied it fast. The forest was being chewed up and it gave me a rush. Throughout it all I could hear Nacho laughing. He loved it just as much as I did. Once I was unloaded, I called "CEASE FIRE." We were only a 150 meters away!!!

Nacho came out from behind the boulder. "Now it's my turn Kidd. Get behind that big rock to your right. Let me know when you're ready." I gave him the thumbs up and disappeared behind this rock on my side of the valley mountain. Nacho opened up and I see all the earth exploding around me. I loved it!!!! After a few minutes Nacho said he was finished. We both met at the valley floor and were laughing our tails off. We loved this type of thing. Now we had to find Huero.

We hiked a mile back to the parking spot where we left my car. Huero was smoking a cigarette cleaning his 45 pistol on the trunk of my car. He saw us coming and shook his head. I asked him what happened. He put his weapon down and said" You guys are crazy. BOTH of you need to be in the psych ward at the VA. I'm NEVER going hunting with you guys EVER AGAIN!!!! Take me home Jim." We started laughing at him. He stuck to his word. He never went hunting with Nacho and I ever again, lol.

I started my claim again in the year 1975. I had been battling my nightmares, flashbacks, and everything that came with it. There was a constant fight. Not to mention the continuous amounts of paperwork to be filled out. They wouldn't get me lost though. I was determined to beat them at their own game. On top of that, I knew that my brothers were getting crap pay like I was. They were also probably going through the same mess I was. I was letting them know what I was going to beat the VA or collapse on my way towards the finish line. They were not getting rid of me that easily. Nor was I going to be in a drug induced stupor to forget about my claim. I was going to be the one laughing at the VA with my middle finger in the air. I was very patient and very driven. This wasn't welfare we were fighting for. This affected our ability to hold down jobs and be better people. The same government we fought for was trying to make us extinct. It pissed me off. I had stamina and I had the heart for a long fight.

There were some things that affected us veterans and ruined a lot of lives. One example that affected me was the lack of sleep. The flashbacks would keep me up all night. I'd try to stay awake all night since I had no desire to sleep. I wanted to sleep minus the nightmares. Then I'd go to sleep and see all the horrors I witnessed in Nam all over. I started to go to work on zero sleep which affected my job performance. I started hurting at work mentality and once home I'd collapse in bed. No kids, no wife, just my bed. It was almost like I was in a catatonic state. My boss at Clark asked me if I was okay. I told him I was having flashbacks from the war. They were keeping me up all night. He just looked at me like a deer in headlights. Unless you were there, nobody would be able to understand. I knew I had to do something about this. I was exploring all avenues but to no avail.

Eventually things at Clark started to get worst. I took some days off and went to the VA demanding some kind of help. They had just started the process of opening some "Vietnam centers" that were dedicated towards helping Vietnam veterans. It was really a good feeling seeing these places starting to pop up at the local VA's. I really can't stress enough on how bad this took me over. It consumed me. Worse than a drug or alcohol addiction. You just couldn't shut it off. If it wasn't bad enough for the flashbacks, when I'd did sleep I'd hear the radio squawk or screams of agony. It was like I was back in Vietnam. I felt like a child hypnotized by the devil himself. I didn't want to talk about my issues since some of the things I did over there were horrendous. War keeps you in limbo. Sometimes not knowing when and where to turn.

The VA kept denying me so I would be there the next day filing a new claim. I saw so many veterans open their mail, see the rejection letter of their claim, and walk off. They'd be mumbling on their way out how they wouldn't be wasting time at the VA anymore. It's exactly what the VA wanted. Anyways I raised hell every time just to let them know I wasn't going anywhere. I was going to be compensated one way or another.

One of the US methods of shrinking the jungle was to spray a powerful mixture of chemical defoliants. This concoction was named "AGENT ORANGE." They called it this name due to its orange-tang color when mixed. They started spraying this shit all over Vietnamese strongholds. It began in 1961, when we just had military advisers helping the South Vietnamese fight the Communists. It was a real "hush-hush" program that the CIA probably concocted. At least that was my guess.

This is the way the spray worked. It was spread out over massive amounts of jungle by plane. It would then eat up and kill the jungle plants. After it would look like barren fields with nothing left. Almost a replay of General Sherman's (scorched earth policy) during the days of the Civil War. Kill everything, burn everything.

The jungle that was sprayed not only killed the foliage. It also made the farmers unable to grow ANY crops whatsoever. The defoliants were so powerful that nothing would work to revive the sprayed areas. Farmers were screwed and so were many people. I read an article about ten years ago. It said the Vietnamese had barely started to grow crops again in the contaminated areas in the year 2005. That's 40 daggone years the land was worthless. Imagine that.

The program was nicknamed Operation Ranch Hand. It was later discovered that the US had sprayed over 4.5 MILLION acres in the land of Vietnam. This was over a period of 11 years between 1961-1972. There was over 19 million gallons of herbicides sprayed. It's an astronomical number but a true one at that. For years the government denied the existence of Agent Orange, Operation Ranch Hand, and the contaminates in it. The mixtures of this garbage was deadly. It contained dioxin which is used for garden herbicides, etc. These usually can be found in your typical weed eaters and ant killers.

They told us since we'd be drinking water out of rivers throughout the country we'd be fine. We'd just have to drop a couple of halazone tablets (salt pills) to decontaminate the water. It would then be safe to drink. What they didn't disclose was it didn't kill the chemical mixture called Agent Orange. You think we'd be drinking gallons of water from contaminated rivers had we known this? HELL NO. But when you're humping the boonies and deep in the jungles, water is your lifeline. It's more valuable than a weapon or your ammunition needed to save you. Water and dry socks in the boonies were the difference between a live grunt and a dead grunt. Period!!!!!

Researchers have shown studies that dioxin and other chemicals causes serious medical conditions. I'll name a few just to give you examples: tumors, birth defects, serious rashes, psychological symptoms, and even cancer. This not only contaminated US troops but tons more of Vietnamese civilians.

These people had to live there. They got it much worse than us. We basically screwed their water and food sources. The government would not admit to the symptoms of this chemical. They even tried to cover it up for years after. They knew it would be hell to explain what was in this chemical. It didn't work out for them.

PTSD stands for Posttraumatic Stress Disorder. This is a disorder that occurs when you witness something devastating or very tragic. I'll name some of these symptoms for you. A life threatening situation such as military combat. Also it could be a serious accident, a natural disaster such as an earthquake or tornado, or a sexual assault in child or adulthood. Get the hint?

PTSD for us combat veterans was gripping. You just couldn't turn it off like a light switch. It was more difficult than that. Besides the regular nightmares and flashbacks, you became detached. Estranged almost. You didn't want to be around big crowds. I can recall hating parties or family events. It would draw out anxiety and I'd feel on edge. I didn't like it. I remember years later while on the tractor, my tire blew. I flashed and leaped out of that thing in a New York second. I snapped out of it and found myself hugging the ground. My crew were laughing their tails off. They didn't know what happened. I was noticing that I'd lose my cool quick. That wasn't like me. I was a naturally loving person. Soon I became a dynamite fuse. Short and would explode in a few seconds. I needed help and I knew other veterans were seeking the same.

The VA wouldn't say we had this nor did they want to. Again they'd see the cash register opening up and didn't want to compensate us. I kept fighting and resubmitting claims about this. I wasn't going down like that. For Vietnam veterans, there was no psychotherapy back then. This was basically "talk therapy" so to say. They also had antidepressants to help out. My views on those were simple: they were NON-EFFECTIVE!!!!!!

I did what a lot of other vets did to deal with this: I became more withdrawn. I didn't want to even spend time with my wife and kids. I wanted to go hide in my closet and lock the door. I just couldn't face this thing alone. I'd get up at 1am and go in the backyard. It almost became my medicine. I tried everything to help and nothing would. There had to be another way. I guess I didn't see how bad I was becoming but my friends did. Mike would also come by to check on me but I wasn't up for horseplay. I remember one time going to the liquor store and getting a bottle of Jack Daniel's. I got so smashed in the backyard yet I still couldn't sleep. I know others dove deep into drugs and alcohol. I even contemplated suicide. I just couldn't leave my kids. I was determined to find the solution. It took me a while but I finally did. Thanks to thousands of other Nam vets like myself filing claims and never giving up, it worked. Well get back to the final results later. As days went by I began going to the Vietnam center. Talking with other vets about my experiences made me feel good. Especially when others would tell similar tales. I started going back to church as I had strayed from the Lord. He sure is a forgiving Lord for always accepting sinners like me time and time again. Always with open arms too.

Chapter 23: Rollin' Solo in a Constant Blur

I had been with Pat for eleven years now. I was at the point of no return. I didn't want to have my kids suffer because of something I couldn't get over. But it was a fib. I kept on living this lie and it was eating me up inside. I was still hanging on to hope that I'd get over this. My kids were 11, 9 and 5 years old. I knew if we didn't make it out of our marriage the kids would pay for it. I felt Pat was selfish when it came to my needs. She just didn't get it nor did she make the effort to. All she did was get pissed off at the situation and make it my fault. Things were going all south real fast and I needed to come up with a solution FAST!!!!!!!The life that we had created was going up in a haze of smoke.

In February 1982, it was officially over. My marriage was gone forever. I would never be there every morning when my kids woke up. I felt bad and worried that my kids would never forgive me. They were too young I thought to understand but I was dead wrong. I remember my daughter coming up to me telling me "Daddy I know you're not coming back." I couldn't lie to her and so I told her the truth. Little Jimmy just stood near the door and stared quietly at me as I packed. I told him things were going to be okay and he just nodded his head. He knew his world as he knew it was over. My youngest Adrian wasn't even there that day. I figured he was too small to understand. Wrong again. I later found out he had a PH.D in divorce matters by a young age. He just kept things to himself. He was a bookworm, a loner. I believe he was looking for an answer to fix his family at such a young age. Years later he would confirm this. It still stings to this day. I was blessed with the best children a father could wish for. They paid for my mistakes and the devastation I left behind. Yet they still love me to this day and have never trashed me for this. Truly God's children.

Pat made it worse when she'd play hurtful games. By this I mean not letting me see the kids, asking for a lot of money, etc. I didn't care if she wanted to tar and feather me in the middle of the San Fernando mall. I'd have gladly excepted. But to screw with my kids and our time pissed me off. On top of that, she wasn't innocent as she claimed to be. I'll leave it at that. I needed to find a place to stay and fast. After about a week, I stayed at my buddy Roland's parents' house. The Ludlows' were awesome people who had a beautiful house in Sylmar. They were avid dog lovers and had two of the most humungous Great Dane's I've ever seen. If you saw them, you'd think they were bears walking inside the Ludlow residence. I enjoyed the peace and tranquility the house had to offer. I started to regroup and stayed faithful going to church. By now I was working at the Post Office in Van Nuys. The one right off the 405 freeway on Sherman Way. I worked as a mechanic on the graveyard shift. The hours sucked but the night went by pretty fast.

My shift would start there around 11pm. I would get a list of broken down vehicles throughout Los Angeles county. One evening I might go to Thousand Oaks. Another evening I might be in downtown Los Angeles. I would go to that particular site and check the vehicle out. If it started great. If it didn't I would have it towed to the Van Nuys yard. By the time I was back in the yard, it would be around 5am. I'd work on the trucks for about 4 hours max. The other half was picking up vehicles with mechanical issues. It was beautiful. I was now divorced, single, and free to do as I pleased. I almost felt free. I was going to start fresh and try my best. I was still a father to my kids and that was my priority one. Second was to get my claim approved by the VA. I knew this would be years more of battle.

I also started going to the VA a lot more. Church started to ask me to be involved more. Once again I was teaching bible studies on Wednesday. I had all the time in the world since I was on the graveyard shift. I also started dating a few clerks (Joanna and Margie) that worked in the front offices. As I would be leaving they'd be coming in since the worked the day shift. I could see where this was going. I wasn't looking for nothing serious. Just playing the field. I'd just gotten divorced.

There are always going to be a million temptations on how to screw up. You fly straight and life is a blessing. You start dabbling in sinful ways away from the Lord, you end up with headaches and a truckload of misery. You can't see clear when he's not in your life. It's all just a blur. I guess you can say that's where I was headed. I was still teaching at the church and attending the Sabbath regularly. But there was also another life I was leading. I started to be sucked into the oodles of women that were offered to me in the workplace. Hell a few of them even wanted to attend church with me. Yeah that wasn't going to happen. They regularly smoked joints and we sometimes shared em'. Someone always had grass. That was my relaxation.

I started to see my kids every other weekend. I remember trying to be amicable to Pat when I saw her. I had no bad feelings towards her. She was a whole different story. I didn't want my kids to see us argue anymore. Sometimes she'd get under my skin though with her snide comments. I ate crow for my kids though. The way I saw it, they were still handling damage control on my behalf. It's the least I could do for them. She would always try to bait me in a screaming match. I'd piss her off by acting cordial to her. I'd spike the ball when I would tell her "I'm praying for you." She was selfish in the fact that in order to make me suffer she was going to make the kids suffer. Now I was no angel by any means. But I tried my best to do what was right and gave my kids unconditional love. When they'd come over for weekends we'd sit on the couch to watch movies. My three kids would all lay surrounding me from every angle. They showed me the same love I showed them. They just wanted to be with me and I did too. I enjoyed every waking moment with them. It made life happier knowing this. One of our favorites was going to the Van Nuys drive-in. I wish those were up like they were before. You couldn't beat those.

One thing was very clear. I had starting drifting from the Lord in a bad way. I wanted and tried to do good. It seems every way I turned, I was knocked down. Sometimes it felt I couldn't do right by any means. If I was doing right in one area, I'd be screwing around on the other side. My mind was completely convoluted. I am being honest in this perspective. I was feeling like the Apostle Peter who had denied Christ three times before. I was losing the one strength that was keeping me together; The Lord.

Chapter 24: Grazin' in The Grass Till The Snow Came

I 'd been smoking dubeys since God knows how long. Maybe I started dabbling with that around 16 years old. I enjoyed the high, the soothing feeling that came with it. I had never been one to hit the hard drugs like LSD, acid, or Quaaludes. I tried it once before maybe but not my choice of drug. Ever since I almost killed that idiot in Lumberton back in my Army days, I never was a hard core drinker. I'd have a few and I was good.

Cocaine was a drug that was taking over lives by the second. It was the drug of choice for many. Most people I knew were already doing it. I think I might've tried it once before if I recall correctly. It just numbed my nose, mouth, and throat area. I never really tried it after until Margie dumped this baggie of cocaine on her coffee table. Before I continue let me explain a bit what cocaine is.

Cocaine is a white, powdery substance that is usually produced in the jungles of Colombia or Bolivia. It is made from coca leaves that are grown by local farmers. Usually these farmers are peasants and live in the high mountains of both countries. The coca is then extracted from the leaves into a coca paste. When the paste is dried it is usually formed into a "bird" or kilo of cocaine. That's 2.2 pounds to be exact. It is usually 90-100% PURE.

You can't just snort pure cocaine since it would stop your heart fast in the event you did too much. It is usually chopped or "stepped" on with cutting agents like lactic powder or baking soda. It not only knocks down the purity but it makes more powder. Hence if you're selling it, more $$$$$ for you. After you snort it you will feel a numbing sensation go from your nose to your throat. It's called" the drip." It gives you a euphoric feeling. It is a recreational drug and a stimulant. Back in the early 1900's during WWI era, Coca Cola actually put liquid cocaine into the soft drinks. This would keep workers awake for longer periods of time. It would keep you going like the Energizer bunny. Nonstop drum beat. You feel me knocking?

There are many pet nicknames for cocaine so I'll try to name a few. A few are blow, white girl, snow, birdie, pow, yayo, and so forth. They are all funny in a sense but the effects are not. I remember the blow Margie had that night knocked me on my butt. It was really powerful. The girls loved doing "snow bombs." This is when you ingest a line through your mouth. Your throat area immediately becomes numb in seconds. I never cared for those. If not cautious, it could grab you under the water. Even if you were a professional or a lowlife it didn't matter. This drug had no boundaries and sucked in everyone. Or almost everyone at least. Doctors, dentist, lawyers, judges, and even cops. I had a few friends who were cops who did blow on occasion. For many it killed their careers.

I remember Margie telling Joanne and I to make sure to drop some water in our nostrils after we snorted. This would send the remaining cocaine stuck in your nostrils down your throat. It would create this awesome feeling. It would also prevent your nose crystalizing like ice. Otherwise you had to dig out of your nose and that hurt like hell!!!!! We ended up staying up all night partying and having sex. THE WHOLE WEEKEND. Unreal. On top of that I missed church. I felt like a dirt bag and promised myself to go to church the next weekend. These were the hidden skeletons in my closet. My personal battle between good and evil. I hated this side of me. After all the Lord had done for me, I still screwed up left and right. Nobody's perfect. I know I was the farthest one from that.

I had my kids the next weekend and we went to church. It felt great to be back and in the swing of things. I felt my best being there amongst my fellow worshippers. We had our afternoon potluck and it went perfect. I excused myself from the table and went to check on the kids who were playing in the playground. All the kids loved that big playground in the back of the faculty building. I went to wash my hands in the restroom. As I was leaving I noticed one of the stalls were occupied in the corner. I heard the occupant making a snorting noise. I knew what that sound was. I walked out immediately thinking "this drug even infiltrated the church members." Who the hell was I fooling? I was one of those morons who was doing it too. I walked out and didn't even want to know who it was. For all I know it could've been our pastor. No I'm not accusing anyone. I'm just saying this drug was the devil's dust and he'd grab anybody willing enough to try it. I tried to be strong but with everything going on I'd find myself dabbling with it often. Weekends only but hell even that was too much. We're only human though. At least that was my excuse and compromise.

I met a group of guys who had started a band together called "the Coolies." They were awesome musicians and were looking for a manager. Also they needed investors to invest in them. I was immediately sold on them and started to get investment money rolling. I also thought that maybe I needed some consulting to run this properly. I met this man named Geraldo who was a financial adviser. He was a Bahamian national and was well spoken. He told me that he would help me with the business aspects. He had connections in the music industry and he produced this too. I met some well know music figures like Quincy Jones. Any doubt I had in my body left that day. Geraldo was the real deal and he was going to show me the ropes. I was going to do this full blast. After a while I was doing this 100%. I quit my job at the Post Office and was a Music manager now. Mind you, I didn't want to be rich and famous. I just wanted to be rich. Pure and simple. I had bills like everyone else, a music group, and kids to raise. On top of that, child support.

I ended up messing with this girl named Laura who was Mexican. She was pretty hot and had two kids of her own named Larry and Teresa. We lived in Van Nuys and would often conduct meetings of business there. We'd have friends our apartment manager and his wife come over when the kids were gone. They were cool people (Amado and Pearl). He was a crazy guy who liked to party. He was very kind though. Pearl was the same. It was a rolling party within our apartments. Money was coming in by the truckload since I had my manager job. It was all going to the business and I could support myself comfortably. Laura had a full time job also so that just worked out perfect. A year later we were married.

The band and I used to get dressed up. We'd hit up local strip bars to find "potential candidates "for our videos we shot. It was a pitch we used to our advantage and it worked like a gem. We usually came out of the place with five to eight strippers. We'd go back to either Steve or "Stereo's" house and have parties while jamming to music. I sometimes called Amado and he'd come join the party. Pearl and Laura would complain but we didn't give a damn. I had more money than I could count, the band was on their way up, and I was leading the charge. We were going to hit the "payola" hell or high water. That's how determined I was. All along I was slipping into darkness worse than before.

The mistake I was making during this time is I started straying away from church. BAD MOVE. The church members would sometimes call the house and I'd have Laura answer. I'd have her tell them some cockamamie stories about how my PTSD was kicking my butt. They all were sincere and prayed for me. They were all well-wishers who put God before anything. The way it was supposed to be. I admired those people for that. Me on the other hand felt embarrassed. I felt ashamed and two-faced. So I did what any coward would do. I stopped going completely. Laura told me we should all go back and start over. I told her to mind her own business. Who the heck was she to tell me my business? She didn't know what I was going through.

We were having dinner and I was about to eat. It was at the apartment. My youngest son was there with Larry and Teresa. Laura served me and whispered in my ear "the devil is winning." I immediately lifted the bowl of hot noodles and splattered it across the den wall. I walked in the kitchen as Laura looked like she saw a ghost. I told Adrian to grab his jacket and let's get out of here. He flew to the room, put on his coat, and said "I'm ready Dad." We left the apartment and got into my Toyota Celica. I lit up a cigarette and told my son "sorry you had to see that son. I shouldn't have lost my cool like that." He calmly responded "its ok Dad as long as you didn't aim that bowl of soup at me I'm fine." He smiled at me and padded my shoulder. "You're still my hero!" I didn't feel like no hero. Ashamed of my actions. The drugs, womanizing, and every other vice was taking over. Even when I felt worthless my kids knew how to pick me up when they didn't even realize it. They are my rock. They have never quit on me. They have never disrespected me.

After three years I lost it all in one shot. Geraldo our trusted financial adviser skipped out of town with all our investors' money. So close to success and screwed right on the spot. The band went their own ways and the anguish marinated in my gut. I had investors to answer to, and now my money source was gone. I wanted to scour the earth looking for Geraldo but didn't have the bankroll to do it. Oh well, lesson learned. I have nobody to blame but myself. If my head was straight I would've spotted his BS.

When your judgment is clouded by drugs and deceitful people, you make weak decisions. You think the smiling faces are there to help you. But it's just a mask these wolves are wearing. Underneath those masks are demented, twisted grins. They are the devil in disguise. It's just how it works. Also my relationship was Laura was over. I found out a few dudes from her work were sleeping with her. I didn't care about that since I was dating women on the side at record numbers. I just used that to walk out and I did. She gave me the finger as I shut the door. That was the last of Laura thank God. I filed for divorce Monday morning. I'd been sliding down "the slopes" for too long. I needed clarity. I needed God back to guide my way. It wasn't going to be an overnight thing as I continued to fail along the way. But I tried as best as I could. I had a ball of blow in my glove compartment. I went inside a McDonald's restaurant to use the restroom. After I took a piss I threw the blow in the toilet and flushed it. Good riddance. Unfortunately, it wouldn't be the last time I saw that junk!!!!!

Chapter 25: Tumbleweeds and Hayseeds

I started working in construction digging pools and landscapes. It was an easy job and I was a wiz on the tractor. My favorite was the Bobcat 943. I could do things in that tractor as though I was riding a bike. I had a good crew with me too. All hard workers who loved the intensity of the job. I had hand-picked these guys off the yards at local lumber yards in the San Fernando Valley. I met this white girl Tanya in a hick bar in Van Nuys called Callahan's. It was by the airport and it was a cool place to "hunt." She went back to my place and she ended spending the night. She was very sexual. A few nights later I took her out to dinner. She had a great body, humorous personality, and was taller than the average. I didn't care. She said she lived in Lancaster an hour north of L.A. She was visiting her sister Layla who lived in Van Nuys. I asked her if she needed a ride back to Lancaster. She accepted my invitation. I ended up taking her back to her place. God what a sorry place that city was. Funny I'm saying that because three months later I moved up here. The things we do sometimes, lol. Six months later we were married.

I moved in with Tanya to Lancaster in 1985. This place was the bionic wasteland. It reminded me of "Bartertown" from the movie Mad Max Beyond Thunderdome. I mean it, there was nothing but desert. It was unreal. The times hadn't caught up with this place. There was a shopping plaza off Avenue L with a movie theater, batting cages, and a few shops. There were places like Apollo Park and Edwards Air Force Base down the 14 freeway. Other than that, it was a bunch of hayseeds who were country hicks. I didn't mind them. They were cool people and never bothered me. It was a different setting but I needed a change. There were housing developments that were being built at a fast flowing number. I was going to get my hands on this. It didn't take long before I had a crew and we were working. Once again BIG money started to roll in. It wasn't hard when you were driven.

We settled in a trailer park on the east side of town. I got my crew ready and plugged into the construction boom. I set my pay along with my crew's pay with the boss Darren. I was getting paid 250 a DAY plus expenses. My guys were making 110 a day. This was killer pay for me and for them. It was all under the table pay too. COLD HARD CASH!!! Cash is king as always. We were rolling in the dough.

Tanya had a really crazy family. I mean they were the fun Beverly Hillbillies and acted like it too. They were first and foremost loving. They might have been a little weird but I enjoyed their company. We would have card games at her brother in law's house that lasted until the next morning. I know what's your next question. Were we using cocaine during this time? Absolutely yes. We'd play card games like highball, lowball, 7-card stud, and strip poker. It was a whirlwind. It wasn't uncommon to see someone fooling around in the room next door. It's just the crazy world we were living in. As soon as 6am rolled around, someone sober enough went to get more booze. It was a crazy time.

At this time church had taken a back seat. The distance also separated how much I saw my kids. Now I am here to be honest and will tell you the truth. My selfish exploits were the cause of this. My ex-wife had a thing to do with it too. But the most part

190

it was me. There were times I just didn't want to deal with Pat. I wanted to see my kids but had to deal with her. She was relentless and selfish when it came to the kids.

When my kids did come here we'd do a lot of things together. I would take them to Eastside pool to swim or to fish at Apollo Park. Around that time the space shuttle would land at Edwards Air Force Base. I loved hearing the sonic boom when the shuttle touched down on earth. It was one of those joys we shared together. Up close the space shuttle was gigantic. We also seen the Voyager parked there. That was that plane that flew around the world.

I used to make rockets with the kids. We'd go launch them in nearby Lake L.A. This was so fun and you had nobody to bother you out there. It would take a day to build and then Sunday was launch days. I'd get just as excited as the kids would. We'd hang out with Tanya's family and all go swimming. Then it would be party time after the kids fell asleep. Someone always had cocaine. Bust out the dollar bill!!!

After four years I had enough of this cowtown and told Tanya I was moving. I wanted her to go with me and she said okay. It was too far from my kids, too far from my VA appointments, and away from my Church. I needed to go back to the valley. We moved to her sister Layla's till we got our own place. That place was nothing but drugs and more women. I remember us adults were all in the house. We were all loaded and playing strip poker. Tanya went to bed and her cousin Pam was playing cards still. She was hot. I mean a body on her. She went outside to smoke in the backyard. I followed her out there. I went around the corner and she was waiting for me. I lifted her skirt and we had hurry sex. She was a freak. After we were done, we went back inside and acted as if nothing happened. I know it was a low down thing to do but damn was she hot. Tanya never found out. Pam knew how to keep her mouth closed. She never said a word.

One thing I had in my favor was my work ethic. I found a construction company and got my old crew back. Now I was making 350 a day cash. My workers were making 150 a day cash. I'd even take the boys to work with me and they loved it. I'd pay them to do the cleanup like sweep the driveways, trash detail, and other odd jobs. They loved it. Once we started we were on fire. There was only one problem. The crew started getting smashed on Friday nights and would come to work worthless. I started giving them "crank" to keep them up and ready to work. I had obligations to the owners. It was my tail on the line. Finally, I told them they'd need to straighten up or I'd can them all. I never had to have another conversation with them again.

One thing Tanya started complaining about was that she wanted a baby. She was 15 years my junior and I could understand where she was coming from. But there was no way I was having a baby at 40. I also had my vasectomy redone after our little blessing came along. I didn't want no more kids. She kept on pressing yet I didn't budge. I don't know if the constant bickering got to me or just everything we were doing. I finally told her we'd talk about it later. Later would come way too soon. After that last talk with her I lost my job, lost everything. It was a great wakeup call though. I stopped doing drugs and concentrated on strengthening my faith with the Lord. I had been away far too long and I needed to bounce back. We were living from the high life now to meager times. Our water and power had been shut off. We'd steal water from the neighbors and take showers in the backyards, lol. Survival 101 at its best.

Then one day I came home from church and Tanya said she was going to visit her mother in Lancaster. She said she was going up there for two weeks. The two weeks turned into four then to eight. She finally fessed up and told me the truth. It was over. I was honestly hurt by this and it stung for a month. I had already seen her stray away from me in a dream I had a week before she decided to leave. The way I saw it, I couldn't give her what she wanted. She wanted to be a parent and I already had that title. She wanted something different and I didn't. She filed for divorce in 1990. Marriage # 3 just hit the pavement!!!! OVER.

The difference is after this marriage failure I stayed true to my word. I did my best to stay on track with the church and threw myself into it 100%. I took my kids with me and started attending Pastor Carter's church in Pasadena. He was a great pastor who was speaking straight from God himself. Some of the things he spoke about have now come to life years later. He was direct on his teachings and was accurate with these.

After six months I had met a new woman named Alicia. I should have never fooled with her but I did. She had two kids Sara and Alex. They were both young at the time. Anyhow I moved in with her a few months later. I tried to be the best I could. It was often a tumultuous relationship. She cursed too much and I didn't. I guess we both should have seen the difference. But we tried our best.

The VA was really being cold and I was still getting a meager 50%. That was ridiculous. Till I met Dr. Joy. There was a difference in Dr. Joy and I could see she wasn't the average VA therapist. She started talking to me in group sessions for PTSD. She told me I had a good case and I was one of her "severe" cases she'd ever seen. I met with the group twice a week at the Vet center. Then a one on one with her once a week. I was telling her how I couldn't hold a job. She told me it would be in my best interest not to get serious with Alicia and not to get married. A few months later we were husband and wife. She was not pleased at all. I'll remember her words when I told her I was married. "You're not ready for this Jim." I would find out in the future she was right.

Chapter 26: Victory Dance and Las Vegas Runs

Around December 1994, I had a meeting as usual with Dr. Joy. She was very pleasant and said if I was ready for our one on one session. I said I was and we were about to begin. Then she paused and rose from her chair. "Jim I told you a while back I'd make sure we'd take care of you. I've seen so many veterans cheated out of help financially and mentally. Your request has received approval. We will also be giving you back pay for the years submitted under your claim. Congratulations Jim. You'll be receiving compensation in full around 30 days from now."

My status was immediately changed to 100% disabled. I was rated 100% for PTSD and would be compensated as such forever. I actually was over 100%. I think I added up to about 170% when all said and done. You can only go up to 100%. I had kicked these guys in the balls. Here's my outlook on my twenty-year battle with the VA. They were not prepared for the many PTSD cases coming back from Vietnam. They did not have the resources. The planning was never there. They did not have the funding nor doctors set up for this. They screwed themselves and didn't consider this fact. Over 3,000,000 Americans served in Vietnam. It is estimated that 25% of that number came back with PTSD. That's over 750,000 cases of PTSD. The VA dropped the ball big time. They failed to convey to us veterans the support we so desired yet never received. I had no sympathy for the VA. Due to their chimpanzee style attention to detail, many veterans gave up or committed suicide. It is the worst atrocity committed on our own. They should be ashamed of themselves!!!!!

I couldn't believe it. My eyes became watery and I hugged Dr. Joy for a minute. She understood my pain and knew I wasn't a fraud case. It had taken twenty years of appointments, rejections, doors slam in my face, to get here. This war back home was worse than the one I'd fought in the jungles of Nam. I've always said that persistence would pay off. It did this time in a huge way. I was to be awarded over 150k!!!! All in one shot. I walked out of the federal building on Wilshire Blvd in West L.A. doing my Victory Dance. I was laughing all the way home. I'd gone face to face with the VA and whooped their behinds. Sooner or later the FROG will get you. I sure did.

Over the next four years I was heading downhill at home. Alicia was going to make me snap and choke her. I had a few strokes in between and medical issues kept coming up. I really believed that she was killing me with her mouth. I had bought a nice house in Mission Hills and it had a pool in the backyard. I knew it was time to go. We were always arguing and hardly got along.

I had suffered a mild stroke being. My blood pressure was through the roof. I needed a change and I knew she wasn't included in that. You can't change certain people who are set in their ways. I told Alicia I was not happy. I told her we just didn't get along and jumped in way too fast. She just agreed and walked away into the den.

Around this time my youngest son Adrian would stay with me on occasion. My daughter Trina was living in New York and Jimmy wouldn't even come over. I'd go to his house in nearby Northridge where it was peace and quiet. I understood his feelings. Adrian stayed over often. He'd grab my car keys and said "see you outside Dad. Let's go to the store. I need cigarettes." As soon as I jumped in the car I knew where we were going. Straight to the bank. I'd pull out 3 grand and jump back in the car. In a few minutes we'd be on the 14 freeway going 80mph laughing our tails off. Headed to our favorite spot: LAS VEGAS.

One thing I can say about going to Las Vegas with my son is we became even closer. He was always close to me and spent a lot of time with me. I guess he was trying to make up for the lost time in his early years. Plus, he wasn't married or tied down in any way. I loved the time with him since he was an adrenaline junkie like me. My kids weren't just my kids. They were also my best friends. I could talk to my kids about anything. When my daughter was younger, she told me FIRST when she got her period, when she started having sex, etc. I was very open with my kids and told them the truth even when it killed them. I remember on one of our many "Las Vegas Runs" Adrian confirmed my thoughts. In his words he always would say" Dad if you ever lied to us and we found out, your credibility would've been shot." I believed him and knew he was right. I'd sometimes go to Las Vegas with Jimmy. We had a good run at the blackjack table one time. Other times we'd pick up my brother Mike. Sometimes it would end up in disaster though. I'll get to that in a minute.

We get to the Stardust hotel and Adrian gets us a room. After that we gambled our butts off. We'd stay up night and day. After a few days we collapsed a blackjack table and massacred them. We walked off with 4 thousand. I decided I'd play all night. Adrian went to bed with his money in his pocket. He knew he'd probably lose it. Also he knew he would be driving us back to Cali since I'd be dead tired. He knew the ropes. Papa always out-ranked him!!!!

With enough money to go around life was more simple. I didn't have to struggle but also Alicia was a spender. I knew I was going to leave the house soon. She could have it all. I just wanted my clothes, car, and medals. I'd regroup and start fresh elsewhere. Just not with her. It was over and I was leaving. She couldn't believe it but I was done. Once I walked out and drove away a 100-pound weight lifted. I wanted out of this relationship. Time to have fun. It was over.

I picked up Mike and told him how it went. He just shook his head as if to say" I told you so." We ended up going to the movies all day. I think we saw all the headliners in one day. Six movies to be exact. Not bad for a $7.50 ticket lol.

I got my own apartment and bounced around with relatives for the next six years. It was a great time and there were many crazy moments I had. I went to the church here and there. Once again the devil was winning. I just wasn't ready to go back full time. I was having a blast yet felt empty inside. I'd occasionally buy a gram of cocaine and have a few "bumps" but nothing major.

Adrian, Mike, and I kept going to Las Vegas over the next five years. I'll tell you one story that sticks out. It was a Sunday afternoon in 2001. Adrian started hinting that we should go up for a few days. The idea seemed good. I called Mike and told him "I had an itch up my ass." I wanted to go gamble in Las

Vegas. I loved the rush, the excitement, and the winnings. Just hated the losing part.

Mike said he was at a Mexican bar drinking. Adrian and I drove over. He was eating some enchiladas and wasn't too buzzed. I told him we'd pick him up in a few hours. When we returned he was piss drunk. I couldn't believe it. When Mike was drunk he could be so damn obnoxious. I wanted to leave him there but Adrian talked me in to letting him go. Once again on the 14 freeway. Off to Las Vegas as usual.

As we passed into Canyon Country I heard Mike gurgling as if he was going to vomit. I told Adrian to pull the car. He wouldn't so I grabbed the wheel and he finally pulled along the shoulder. I got off and threw Mike out of the car. I made him cough up whatever he needed to. He said he didn't have to throw up. He got in the backseat and we drove off.

Once again he started saying he was sick. We pulled off the next exit into a Denny's restaurant. Mike went to use the restroom. After 10 minutes I sent Adrian in to check on him. He came out laughing a minute later. I assumed all was well and went to investigate. Adrian tells me "Dad go look at Uncle Mike. He's fine." I walked into the restroom and Mike was upbeat. He was washing his face and picked his head up. He smiled and said "Hey Kidd I feel better." Then I saw the urinals and floor full of barf. I lost my dinner outside right after. God I hated seeing that nastiness. They'd set me up good. I had bit hook, line, and sinker. Mike fell asleep the rest of the way till we reached Las Vegas. A few years later Adrian moved up there permanently.

He still resides there today. I guess the bug never left him, lol. All about the action. All about the dollars.

In December 2003 my biological mother Bertha passed away. It hit me really hard especially since our last years, we were estranged. She had her way of thinking and I had mine. It was just the way it was. I had made peace with her a long time ago yet I still hurt. I left my house I was at and went to a local liquor store. I was walking around town drinking a fifth of Jack Daniel's when I heard a car pull up. "Dad is that you?" It was my son Jimmy. He asked me if I was okay and I broke down. I was distraught, confused, hurt, pissed off, and felt all other emotion you could imagine. I had them flooding my heart at once. My heart just bled tears and I had no ability to fix it. I spent the rest of the evening smoking cigarettes and talking with Jimmy. He made me feel so much better after. We prayed together and I hugged him before he went home. I never even called him. Just like I knew when my kids were in pain, they knew the same with me. He went looking for me and found me on that dark street in Mission Hills. I can't convey to you enough how wonderful my children are. I love them so much. They're my world.

Chapter 27: Three Straight Knockdowns!!!!!

Since I had taken the VA to school my next agenda was to get my brothers compensated. All of three of them. Nacho was one who was still getting 30% and Cirilo was getting 40%. Mike was only getting 60% and still holding down a full time job. I didn't want that to continue. I saw the opening and I had created the blueprint to win. Nacho was stubborn and kept balking until he opened up one day. He was one who suffered the most from PTSD. He kept his family in seclusion, booby-trapped his own house, and would patrol his yard. I think he finally acknowledged he could use the extra bread. He started listening to me and going to the VA. He stayed true to his appointments and I made sure he was on point. Then came hard times for him. He went homeless.

After bouncing around from the streets to family members houses for a year, he finally received word that he would be rated to 100%. He called me up ecstatic and said he would be receiving back pay as well. "I told you Kidd. You have it made now. You deserve this." Within two months, Nacho moved his family to a beautiful two-story house in Victorville. It's a small town 90 miles Northeast of Los Angeles. He also bought a nice van equipped with plenty of room for the family. He furnished the house very nice and threw a little party. He always cooked the best food, had unlimited alcohol, and would get me to smoke grass with him. Nacho smoked DAILY and FAITHFULLY. He'd wake up and go downstairs. He'd start the coffee and sit in the middle chair of his oak table. He'd break out his pipe and put a paper towel under it. Then it was to the refrigerator to get his grass. He kept his grass wrapped in a plastic Ziploc and foil. He had this method that he'd cut an orange peel and put it in the grass. It kept it moist. It worked. Also he was relishing in the benefits of the VA. He never had to worry anymore financially. His youngest son Michael even went to a local college and got paid for it. What a win!!! I wasn't finished yet though.

The next one that started to follow the process was Cirilo. He started going to his appointments and refiling dead claims. We used every angle we had to. It was us against them. We were owed these benefits and needed them. About two years later Cirilo called me up. I knew we'd kicked them in the balls again. He too had won his case. Here comes his 100% and back pay within 30 days. It was beautiful to hear and to see. I was not going to take a backseat and watch my brothers suffer in pain. We already had witnessed things that were atrocious. We weren't trying to rob the VA. We only asked what we had coming to us. The US Government never had to look for us. We volunteered to fight for our country because we had pride. We had honor. They should've taken care of us better than this!!!! I guess later is better than never right?

The last one to receive his 100% was Mike. Now Mike's was going to be a big blast to them. Mike never went to Vietnam but fought a bigger war within. The VA had found his Hodgkin's disease in 1970 when he was just 19. After he went through years of body scorching treatments, it left him weak. It left his body permanently altered. His bones in his shoulders and neck protruded immensely. That would never be normal. When he went into "spontaneous remission" he still had to live. He worked his whole life as a wallpaper hanger and painter. He had a family to support. Now as he grew older, he couldn't perform the basic duties that came with the job. He needed compensation and I was going to be the one to help him get.

We also went after for back pay since he was dated years back with the disease. We were going full blast and I walked with him each step of the way. There were times were Mike would procrastinate and miss appointments. I remember he missed one crucial meeting. I called him in the afternoon to see how it went. He told me he missed the appointment. I BLEW A GASKET!!!!!

"WHAT DO YOU MEAN YOU MISSED IT? WHAT'S WRONG WITH YOU KIDD?" Simple response came from Mike. "Jim shut up. I know what I'm doing. I'll just reschedule for next week. Stop your whining." He just didn't get it. He thought the VA waited hand and foot. They didn't and they loved when this would happen. I finally told him "alright I'm done" and hung up the telephone. He tried calling back but I shut my phone off. I couldn't conceive the thought of turning your back on money that was owed to you. All you had to do was follow procedures by the numbers and you'd be a winner!!!!

A few hours later Mike was at my front door knocking. I told him he was a fool for gaffing this appointment off. I told him he could go through his own file and make his own calls to the VA. I didn't have a worry in the world. I was 100%, Nacho was 100%, and Cirilo too. We were all taken care of. We all had PTSD and Agent Orange symptoms we continued to fight. Mike was still suffering from years of treatment. I just wanted him to live on easy street and relax. He started getting short of breath easier. He was still working around chemicals from the paint. I told him "keep on working and you'll be collapsing on the ladder. Don't listen to me. I don't give a hoot. It's you that's suffering Kidd not me." Mike told me he would follow up on every appointment going forward. He promised not to balk and be on point. From then on we would be blessed again.

They went on to compensate Mike 100% in 2009. It was the final blow. I bet the VA had a hit-squad after me for the collateral damage I inflicted. I didn't care for them. They didn't have compassion for us who had problems, REAL problems. So we went even a step further. We went to get Mike compensated even further. The VA was in a lose-lose situation. I loved having them behind the eight ball. Had they taken the right steps to veterans like us we might have been calm about this. But for those of us who fought in the hells of Vietnam, it was embedded in us. I never had anything given to me and we were always the underdogs. I loved it. I loved it when people counted us out. One thing you don't do is count us out. We'll come back in a wave harder than a tsunami hits.

I started to get my head together and concentrate on church. I became increasingly involved and worked hard at this. I was determined to foster my energy into this. I needed to be surrounded by the Lord and his ways. I'd fell off and on for so long. I'm only human. I never claimed to be a saint. Even when I wasn't in church, I'd have a kind heart. The only time my heart turned black was when I had to fight the VA. I had no reservations when it came to these cold hearted animals. That's just the balls out reality of it. As I mentioned earlier, I tried my best. The devil can be relentless though. It seemed when you tried to do right, the devil lurks more and more. Yet the Lord is always stronger.

207

Chapter 28: High Stakes Gambling

After a fifth failed marriage to a woman I had no business with, I went to live in Ontario with my sister Mary. We'd always had a good relationship and stayed close. Her boyfriend Miguel was a nice guy who put up with her shit lol. I tell you, Mary wasn't weak. We'd have constant BBQ's where most of the brothers and sisters would come over. We'd play music and have drinks till the wee hours. Miguel would make some killer homemade chile'. My niece Helen would make some great platters of prosciutto with cantaloupe. It was a great time. I moved into the back portion of the house. It had its own bathroom, living room, TV, and a small fridge. Peace and tranquility. After a while we'd have karaoke on a consistent basis. Having family around was great. Mike used to come from his place in San Diego and spend at least a week with me every month. As usual, temptations were always there. I begin to fall into one of my old vices: GAMBLING.

Now Ontario is about 15 miles to Interstate 15. If you jump on northbound 15 from the 10 freeway, you'll end up in Las Vegas. If you jump on southbound 15 you'll end up in San Diego. Since 1995, Native American tribes of all sorts started gaining interest in casino gaming. They had one casino in the small town of Cabazon called Morongo. It was a nice casino 55 miles east of Ontario. We'd all take trips down there and gamble away. Sometimes we'd win but most of the times we got our butts handed to us. Just stating facts here.

By the year 2009, they were all over the place. From Soboba casino in Yucaipa to San Manuel casino in nearby Highland. That was only a 30-minute drive. An hour south on the 15 in Temecula took you to Pechanga casino. That resembled a Las Vegas casino for sure. They all started upgrading and it was easy access. I had a steady income coming in and I started visiting these places quite often. It wasn't about the rush anymore. It was all about the win. Rarely do casinos watch people smash jackpots. They frown on it. The smart casinos let more win to draw bigger crowds of gamblers. The comps started going out and here came the people. I didn't give a damn about comps like free bingo, meals, rooms, etc. I cared about winning. One night winning I did in a huge way. Let's get to that story.

It was June 2010 on a summer evening. I had just got my VA monthly check and headed to San Manuel casino for a little action. I loved playing keno the most. Keno was a game where you picked 2-10 numbers out of 80 numbers. If you played a 5 spot and hit all 5, on a quarter bet it would pay $208 dollars. I would usually go for the gusto and play a 7 or 8 spot. I would also crank up the bets so I was playing anywhere from1-3 dollars A HAND. Yeah I know, it can get steep quick. I had to go big or go home. That was my motto.

I was playing for about four hours and it was late into the wee hours already. I had won around $1,200 dollars and continued my roll. I was determined to hit a few more bucks before I called it a night. I lit up another Marlboro and hit the play button. All of a sudden in slow motion, the pay chart started dropping. My numbers kept hitting till it hit the bottom. JACKPOT BABY!!!!!!!!!!!!!!!! AN 8 SPOT FOR 20 LARGE!!!!!! Yes, 20 thousand dollars on a $3 8-spot. I couldn't believe it. I was in shock and overjoyed. It was going to do me a lot of good. I had extra money now. The attendant came over and said "wow that's an awesome hit sir." She took down my information and my player's card. She told me she'd be back since the win had to be verified. I told her no problem and that I wasn't going anywhere.

I started playing the machine next to mine. I played an 8 spot at a $1.50 a hand. Within ten minutes the unthinkable happened: I HIT ANOTHER JACKPOT!!! This time for 10 thousand dollars. This was surreal. My jaw dropped to the floor. I composed myself and waited for the attendant to pay me out in full. I didn't have to fill out a tax form either since I was exempt. 100% disabled. My favorite Uncle Sam wouldn't be getting his hands on this booty. I walked out of the casino with the biggest Kool-Aid smile on my face.

It was adamant on getting a hold of my kids. I was going to help them out. I called them up and they all answered in the middle of the night concerned. I sent each one $5,000. I was happy to be able to help them. They were just as thankful. I then called the airlines and booked a flight to New York City the following day. I was going to visit my daughter Trina for a week.

A week later I arrived in NYC's John F Kennedy airport. Trina was waiting for me and we embraced. I spent the week traveling the state with her and catching up. She told me how she was working at a car dealership and took me there. She introduced me to all of her co-workers. We'd go to different restaurants every evening for dinner. It was time well spent. After a week my time came to return to California. We hugged and kissed each other goodbye. I got on the plane that day so content. I mean, I only had my son Jimmy living in Northridge, CA. Trina had been on the East Coast for almost 20 years by now. Adrian was in Las Vegas, Nevada for 7 years by now. He was only a four-hour drive away. Trina on the other hand was a five-hour FLIGHT away. Either way the distance was greater than it showed. But I had to support them and their decisions. They were both flighty. They wanted to go and explore more than the average. I knew they'd never come back to live in California. Turns out I'd be wrong on one of them. We'll talk more about that in a bit.

I made the remaining money last as long as I could. I started going out to the casinos every weekend now. I started gambling full blast. I was determined to smash out another jackpot. Greed at its best. I also began to hit the nightclub inside San Manuel. I met this hot Cambodian broad named Soon. She had a drop dead body for being 60 years old. Nice perky breasts and a rock solid bosom. Beautiful jet black hair to the top of her butt. I asked her to go out with me. She ended up coming home with me that night. It definitely wasn't her first rodeo. She knew the ropes!!!!

Soon wasn't the only woman I'd be dating. I was meeting more and more women there. I also started going to a karaoke bar in West Covina called "The M." Another meat market. A few of my brothers came with me to get on the action.

This consumed my entire time. I didn't really care to do much else but go gamble. I wasn't going to church at all nor was I reading the scriptures. My bible became encrusted with an inch of dust. I knew I was screwing up and just wanted to hide. I even did a few lines of blow with some of these broads. I was sliding downhill at a record speed. I just didn't want to end the fun. Well, fun then turned to complete misery. It started to be a stress box and now I HAD to win all the time. My winnings were down to a few grand and I was hoping for one more jackpot. It never came. I remember spending my ENTIRE VA check in one freaking night. Yes, ONE. I had bills and rent to pay. I did what any person with a problem has: I borrowed it.

It became a point after a while that I was borrowing half of my VA check to gamble. Shit got really bad when you didn't have a dollar bill to eat a hamburger. The only thing I was doing was smoking three packs of cigarettes a day. The doctor had warned me to stop smoking but I didn't listen. The kids told me to slow down and get back in the church. I still didn't listen. I thought to myself "I can stop anytime if I wanted to." Truth was I couldn't. I just didn't care to admit it. I knew they were all right. I'd shut my phone off when I was gambling. The kids weren't fooled. Either was family members. I started having doors slam in my face. Not because they wanted to. I had forced them too. I recall a time I asked for a loan from Adrian. He asked me what it was for. I told him for food. He said "I'll send you a gift card. You better not sell it for cash either. Make sure you eat Dad. "

I had put everyone in a bind and it was my stupidity that caused this. I have no excuses and I am remorseful for my actions. It finally hit me hard and I stopped going to casinos altogether. I even had San Manuel casino voluntarily "86" myself out of there. I didn't want to be around that environment anymore. I started ignoring these women I met too. I just had to clear my head. I had to rebuild my relationships with my kids and my family members. Most of all I had to be close to God. I had taken it too far this time. I was again lost without him in my life.

I made a promise that I would be faithful to him and his word again. I was not going to bend no matter what.

I still drop in a casino once in a blue moon. I'll only go in there with $40 and that's it. I have things under control and don't get out of hand. But those occasions are few and far fetched. I'd be consumed in the church and happily so. I remember that Friday evening getting my suit and slacks prepped. I had a big day coming. I'd be once again walking in the house of God. I couldn't wait. I was in a blur for a few years. The year was now 2013. I was coming back clear and strong. God does miracles when you least expect it.

Chapter 29: My Ultimate Comeback on the Road to Glory

The most difficult thing we as humans have trouble doing is admitting we have a problem. It is the uncovering of our guilt and wrongdoings. We hate feeling like rubbish since we know the covers are pulled off our faces. The end result though is beautiful once you face your demons. I felt so charged up that March 2013 Saturday morning. I woke up around 530am and prayed for an hour straight. I flew in the shower, got dressed, and was out the door. I headed to my favorite coffee shop "Joanne's "to have breakfast. It was a nice meal of oatmeal, turkey bacon, and sourdough toast. I loved their coffee there too. It was off to church. I entered the church parking around 10am and noticed fellow church members arriving. I recognized a few of them. I was back where I needed to be. In God's house.

The ironic thing was I wasn't forced to go back. I wanted to go back to church so bad. It was such a cleansing when you went to church and listened to the word of the Lord. It not only kept you on an even keel, it made you do so much better. No human being is perfect. God knows this and understands. But that doesn't give us consent to go buck wild by any means. I always took note of one thing. When I was away from church, I was Satan's helper basically. When I walked hand in hand with God, life's gifts came to me by the truckload. My soul was illuminated with God's love. Life would always be that much better. It has always been our choice to choose right or wrong. God always gives us the chance to choose wisely. Whether we do that or not is our own failure or win.

Mike also became a regular at my church. He took it in with open arms. I loved the fact that he wasn't close minded. Mike really embraced the church and saw what it really was. It was for everyone who wanted God in their lives. We had 80-year old people to 18-year old gangbangers. Every person knows what he lacks in his heart and soul. Some wake up and do something about it. Others do nothing and die in eternal hell. It's just that simple.

Mike started giving his input about the lesson we had to study in Sabbath school. The church members were amazed by his in depth knowledge of the bible. I can still picture Mike walking in with his bible. He had so many highlighted pages, cliff-notes, and notes sticking out of numerous pages. It was amazing since this wasn't Mike's home church. But he made such a deep impact with the members they kept asking him to teach. He obliged and kept coming back. It made me feel excited every Saturday knowing my brother Mike would be going to celebrate with me. Going to church on the Sabbath was always a celebration. It was the Lord's celebration and we gave thanks to him. It was all his glory. All the praise went to him.

As I stated earlier in this chapter, good things start to happen when you walk side by side with the Lord. One thing that amazed me was how much my son Jimmy took into the church. He'd had a rough three years due to a few knee surgeries. He'd been out of work due to his injuries for quite some time now. But he came almost faithfully and I could see his attitude start changing for the better. He was in tuned with the Lord through good times and bad. It helped him throughout his rehabilitation and his financial struggles. He rarely missed nor did I. I was hooked and feeling my best. Nothing was going to get in my way. I started going over to Jimmy's place more often. We'd read the bible together and talk in detail. It was beautiful. He was learning more than he ever had before about the Lord. He was enjoying the pastor and his teachings. He was also making new, honest friends at church. The people at our church are so kind hearted. God is great in so many ways!!!!!!!!!!!!!

I remember my youngest son Adrian flew in to Los Angeles from Las Vegas. He wanted to visit me and I asked him if he'd attend church with me that morning. He was more than happy to. I picked him up at LAX and we headed out. He was dressed in his church clothes and happy to see me. We stopped by for breakfast and then headed to my church. It was already crowded there and the choir started singing religious notes. Their voices were so beautiful. The pastor went about his sermon. It happened to be about death. Something I was well versed in. The pastor then did something I hadn't seen him do in a while. He asked the church members to welcome and pray for the Devine family. They were seated in the front row right hand corner. Mr. Devine was a church member here for many years. He had passed away from natural causes at the age of 82 the day BEFORE. His wife was sitting next to their children and grand-children in the front row. He invited Mrs. Devine to say a few words. She thanked everyone for their support and gave praise to the Lord. Here was a woman who just 24 hours ago lost her husband of 58 years. The very NEXT day she is in church. Just as she sat down, we looked on. We were in amazement.

Just then Adrian leans over to me and says" Dad that is a true angel there. I don't know if I'd be in church the next day if Sugar (his wife) passed the day before. She's a better person than me.

217

But that shows the power of faith, the power of the Lord Dad. Amen to that." He had stolen the words right out of my mouth. When we lose loved ones we are often paralyzed in a state of shock. Almost like life stops. Everything hurts too. Yet if your faith in God is strong, he'll breathe strength and willpower into your body you never knew existed. It is a fact. I've seen it time and time again.

I get a telephone call six months later from my daughter Trina. She was still residing in New York. After a few minutes of small talk, she tells me" Daddy I'm coming home. I need to be around family. I miss you guys." Before I became flattered with joy, I stopped myself. I had seen this move from my daughter a million times. Then again, I realized I had been praying for her to come back to California. She sounded different this time and asked me if I could help her move back. I told her if she was serious that I would fly out to New York. Then I'd drive back the 2,700 miles with her to California. My cousin Sylvia went with me. She helped cover most of the expenses. She made the trip possible. She was an angel sent from Heaven. She has a heart of gold.

Three weeks later I was on a JetBlue flight from LAX to NYC. Trina picked me up and we went to dinner at an Italian restaurant. The very next day we were on the road back to California. I was so happy she was finally coming home for good. We were driving across the state of Ohio on Interstate 70. Trina cut in front of a truck she couldn't see. The next thing I know, the truck was crushing into the car. We were in a bad accident. They needed the jaws of life to cut us out. We were hospitalized for six days. After two days of recovery, we were in a rented car on our way to California. Some trip so far huh. Nothing ever went as planned when it came to Trina. But she was on her way home with her Papa. That's all that mattered. God had kept us safe even in the nasty car accident. Now we were finally home three days later. She dropped me off at my house and went home to her Nana's house. Once I was home I took a long bath. I needed to massage my back. I could still feel the pain. I called the VA and booked an appointment for Friday. My back was killing me by then. Saturday I was sitting in church with Jimmy. Nothing was going to deter me from hearing the word and giving God praise. NOTHING!!!!

Once in a while in the weeks following, I'd invite Trina to church. She came with me a few times but then her work schedule changed. She had received an immediate job offer from a local car dealership. She ended up working six days a week. She would spend quality time with her mother and grandparents. Jimmy continued to attend church. Mike also attended. Life was flowing in the wind. I felt like I had a new set of wings. My faith was at its strongest. Usually when this happens God will test your faith. I would be tested to its highest level real soon. I would face the heaviest losses yet since my days in Vietnam.

Thanksgiving and Christmas went very good. I went to spend time with Trina and Jimmy down in the San Fernando Valley. Adrian was staying in Las Vegas and not coming down this year. He often told me he never got homesick while traveling the world with the Marines. But he got homesick when he left Las Vegas each time. Las Vegas was his home no doubt.

2015 got off to a rocky start. My oldest brother Nacho had been visiting the VA in and out for the last month of 2014. By the time January 2015 was in the books, he was a steady patient in the VA's Wadsworth hospital in Westwood. His body was deteriorating as each day passed by. He was a fighter and even though we'd been estranged for some years, I went to visit him often. His boy Gilbert and his wife Armida never left his sight in four months. The only time Gilbert or Armida left was to go home and shower. Then they'd return the following day. I respected them a ton. Soon it became evident that the doctors' hands were tied. There wasn't much they could do for him. The pain was so strong and it was increasingly brutal to witness. They started talking to us about his options. They were slim.

Watching someone you knew your whole life stronger than a rock became shrinking like a prune, it's the ultimate worst. I can't convey this enough to anybody who has not witnessed this up close and personal. It is so defeating and helpless that it's hard to imagine that's the same person. Here was our hero who we had grew up with. He was on the brink of death. He made it clear that he didn't want to die. He wouldn't have a choice in that matter as nobody does. We all braced for the worst. The worst soon arrived with a vengeance. I clung to my bible harder than ever. My faith would get me through this whatever way it played out.

Chapter 30: A Trail of Tears Down Lonely Street

As we thought, Nacho's health worsened and they gave him a few days to live. True to Nacho's fighting capabilities, he lasted 13 days with minimal pain medications. He refused most towards the end. I know Kidd probably wanted to take one more blast before he passed on. He loved his grass.

On May 27th 2015, my brother Nacho passed away. He was always strong and very patriotic. He didn't embrace a lot of things he should've but he lived his way. Right or wrong. He did a lot of things for the family and his younger siblings. He had a beautiful ceremony at the Riverside National Cemetery in Riverside, California. They played "taps" and then whisked his casket away for a private burial. That was the way they performed military services at Riverside. A rep from his unit the 173rd came to pay his final respects to a fallen sky soldier. This was unreal. In one shot, my oldest brother was called by God. Just like that.

During the following weeks I kept digging into the God's word and staying true to myself. I often found myself doing a lot more volunteer work for the church. It consumed me in such a good way. I was still feeling the effects from my brother's passing. But God and certain family members kept me going on the straight path. Seeing my oldest son Jimmy in church was always a pick me up. I loved how he embraced the word and how he kept changing for the better. Just like I was. My kids always would tell me in their own words "when you're involved in the church you're UNSTOPPABLE." I loved that feeling of power. That came from the Lord. My worst enemy ALWAYS was ME. Hands down.

After the summer was over I received a telephone call from my ex-wife Pat. She told me that Hanky wasn't doing too good health wise. He had multiple heart surgeries over the last 10 years and his smoking had worsened his health overall. He really was doing worse than I thought when I went to visit him in September at UCLA medical center. I prayed that he'd make a full recovery but in my heart I felt his time on earth was winding down. Hanky was not my foster brother. He WAS my brother. Hanky and I had a special bond most didn't even know about. I'll always be grateful for him saving my life during my first firefight. He put himself in the line of fire to protect his little brother. What balls he had. I'll never forget him visiting me in a Vietnam field hospital after I got hit. He made me feel so good inside. He was also very good to my children. He was both my boys' Nino and he was extremely close to them. Adrian and Jimmy had become closer through the years.

Hanky had brash ways and an "I don't give a damn who gets offended" attitude. But in his last five years he was changing his ways for the better. He tried to repair damaged relationships with his kids and friends. He went as far as taking a trip to Vietnam to heal wounds. I remember him telling me he went to his old camp and battle sights. He dug a hole, buried a pack of cigarettes, and poured a beer for the boys.' He came back more alive I'd say. That took some balls of steel to do something like that. You couldn't get me to go back there. Too much pain, too much damage. Maybe one day but I'm not ready for that now. I heard many Nam vets doing this and healing for the better. Closing wounds as they would call it. We never stop seeing war out of our eyes. PERIOD.

I told my son Adrian that I didn't know if his Nino would make it much longer. I could see as each time we visited him, he looked weaker. Dad was in his 80's and looked healthier than he was. Adrian and Sugar flew in on Christmas Day. They went to visit him with Pat at UCLA Medical Center. They spent a few hours with him and then left. Adrian told me he'd never see his Nino alive again. He knew it. I could see his pain and my kids spoke reality the way I did. We were always on the same frequency. Even when it killed us inside. His condition started plunging downhill. Jimmy and I went to visit him frequently. His time was ending. His kids Monique and Hanky Jr were there constantly. I don't recall a time when I went to visit him and one of them weren't there. They have my utmost respect for that.

On Tuesday February 9th 2016, Henry Armen Medellin (aka Hanky) passed away peacefully as we all stood by. The room was crowded and we all were there for him. I remember the day before his daughter Monique told him they were taking off the breathing apparatus. She showed strength and poise during this rough time. I was proud of my niece and nephew. He had a beautiful service along with the 21-gun salute and "taps." I was honored that his kids choose Jimmy to read at his funeral. Adrian was chosen to be one of his pallbearers. He wore a 101st Airborne Division jersey in his Nino's honor. Memories of Hanky filled my head. I had a blast with that guy. He was a character who just didn't care. This was a hard pill to swallow. Devastation would land in our lap less than 24 hours later. Talk about test of faith. God was going to push me to the brink of insanity.

The very NEXT day was Wednesday February 10th 2016. I was headed to San Diego to visit our brother Mike. He wasn't doing too well either and was in the VA in San Diego. When I arrived there, I went down to get some coffee from the cafeteria. I received a phone call. It was my sister Juanita. She was crying. I asked what had happened. She told me our younger brother David Ojeda had been killed in a car accident. WHAT THE HELL. ARE YOU KIDDING ME? I couldn't believe this!!!! Back to back I had lost two brothers in 24 hours. I was floored. I let Mike know immediately. They were speechless. One thing we did do was cry and comfort each other. Mike led us in prayer and I told Mike we had to leave. I felt empty. I'd just left Pomona and now headed right back. I was dealing with most of Mike's surgeons and doctors. Now this. I just couldn't wrap my head around this. I couldn't believe he was in a car accident. David was a city bus driver for 25 plus years. He was the type that wouldn't go past 70 mph on our way to Las Vegas. He was the safest driver I met. It turned out he had a heart attack on his way home. He had just received his ashes at his local church that morning. Since he retired six months ago, he'd been actively involved in his church.

He was also feeding the homeless, doing church activities, and running a local karaoke joint. He had a nice girlfriend named Mia who was by his side. He was also a grandfather to his son's kids David and Richard. He loved taking care of them and spending time with him. I loved hanging out with my brother David. He was always trying to compete with us at the karaoke bars. It was fun and he was a riot. I was going to miss him dearly. His service was beautiful and many co-workers from the transit line showed up. He was well respected and had a lot of friends. It was not easy but we tried our best to recover. Through it all, I never missed church. I only missed it that Saturday we buried David (aka Cactus) as he was called. He was most proud of his two kids, his work, his grandkids, and being a "Boulder Rocker."

After this, I started concentrating on my brother Mike's health issues. We were considering them moving him to Riverside VA. That way I would be able to spend time with him each day. He lived with his son Mikey and daughter in law Alma in San Diego for the last five years. I just wanted him closer so I could be there and communicate with his doctors better. We went over this when a ton of bricks hit us. AGAIN!!!!!!!!

Mike's surgeon had my personal number in case his status changed. I had given all the doctors my personal number. I was to be called for any matter. Dr. Glass called me from the San Diego. He was Mike's doctor who I spoke with regularly. I was there the next day with Mike. Dr. Glass walked in. He sat down next to us and begin to speak. His voice was one that was somber and heartfelt. I knew the worst was coming. "Miguel, we have tried all we can do. There are spots on your lungs and it has spread. We recommend you go to the hospice here. I'm very sorry. There's nothing else we can do."

Mind you this was a month after I lost two of my brothers. Nacho had been gone for 10 months and we were still reeling from his passing. Mike was my closest brother. I had just had a ton of boulders fall right on my feet. I felt my world crashing all over but harder than ever. I leaned over to Mike who looked a bit confused. "Kidd did you understand what the doctor was telling you?" He turned his head slowly and said "yeah I think so." I told him the doctor said he was dying and they didn't give him much time. Mike looked at me and said "okay Jim whatever we have to do. Let's pray together. "

We had a heartfelt prayer and cried together. I held hands while praying and I told him I loved him. He told me the same. Mike being himself always gave praise to the Lord. He slightly chuckled saying "Hey I made it this far. I can't complain except give God thanks for giving me 45 extra years." He was right. Mike beat the odds long time ago. He had no fear. He carried a shield of the Lord in one hand and the Bible in the other. He had no fear since God was on his side. We prepared everyone for the unthinkable. Mike would be passing soon.

His kids were all there as were mine minus Adrian. We all stood the last week with Mike until he passed away on Friday March 19th 2016. He passed away at 4am. Adrian and Sugar flew in later that day as did our buddy Roland. We all met up at Mikey and Alma's apartment in San Diego. We all were there for Mike's kids. I could feel their pain but they showed immense composure. During the time he passed away to the day of the funeral, I was so proud of Marie, Mikey, Gabriel, and Matthew. As we were there at the apartment telling stories about Mike, I told everyone I had to go. Adrian asked where I was going. I told him I needed to go to church tomorrow morning. I remember his next sentence verbatim. "I don't know if I could do that Dad. You're a better man than I am." I then asked if he remembered Mrs. Devine. He knew exactly what I was talking about. The lady two years ago who lost her husband of 58 years and was in church the next day. I had to go and give praise to God.

Now I know what you're thinking. Praise? Yes, praise and I'll explain why. Mike should've passed away 45 years ago. He had been blessed with wonderful kids. He was a second father to my kids. He went on wild expeditions with us across the US. I was not going to be selfish and ungrateful. I was going to give thanks. Mike would've done the same if the roles were reversed.

His funeral was one of beauty yet heartbreak. My two sons and Mike's three sons made up the pallbearers. This was awesome seeing my kids and nephews walk him out one last time. They held a gun salute and played "taps" for him. This one drove me to the edge, literally. But I knew Mike was at peace. He never feared this day. He was a warrior of the Lord. It hurt knowing I wouldn't see Mike on this earth again. But we both knew we would see each other again in the Kingdom of Heaven one day.

All the shenanigans we pulled started flowing in my mind. All the times we beat the crap of each other to the hard times we both endured in our many hospital stays. All the times we got to be kids together, all the times we read the scriptures together. Mike and I might as well of been twins. He was my right hand man. Hands down. He was there when nobody else was. He helped out when he lived with Pat and I back in the 70's.

Our remaining siblings for the most part have become closer after all these deaths in our family. We continue to try and help each other. Especially for the nephews and nieces whose fathers are gone. I think back and notice one thing: life sure goes by fast when you never leave the fast lane. It really does. For some they wouldn't understand this. For us, it's just another day at the office. No matter what these four will never be forgotten. My brothers. They are always in our hearts. We will all be reunited when the second coming of Christ happens. Eternal life is the ultimate goal. It should be everyone's in my opinion. We'll never forget our fallen brothers.

Ignacio Nunez (US ARMY /173RD ABN DIV/ VIETNAM 69')

Henry Armen Medellin (US ARMY/101ST ABN DIV/ VIETNAM 67-69')

David Ojeda (MTA UNION REPRESENTATIVE)

Miguel Julian Nunez (US ARMY/ 4TH ARMORED DIV/ GERMANY 69-70')

REST IN ETERNAL PEACE BROTHERS!!!!!!!!!!!!!!!!!!

Chapter 31: Bouncing Back: One Day at a Time

In the time that has passed since we buried my brother Mike, life has been up and down. I went through a horrific bout of depression and despair. I have snapped out of that by the love of my family. Adrian came by last week. He told me I'm not the same and he understands why. We are all hurting from this devastating year. By the grace of God, he heals all. I have no doubt. I dove head first into my church and my readings. That has been the difference in me today. I teach bible studies Tuesday evenings when my Pastor John Aitken can't teach. I faithfully attend church every Saturday morning. I haven't missed one yet. I don't have plans to either.

The love that I have endured by my children is beyond the moon. They are constantly with me in my heart. I have received surprised visits from all three on multiple occasions. We have gone out and embraced each other deeply. We talk on the phone all the time. I see Trina and Jimmy more since Adrian is still in Las Vegas. But I never feel separated at all. We are all very close to this day. Spending time with my children even as an adult is something I seek more and more of. To any parent who is lacking in that department, I tell you to repair that immediately. Our children and the love they bring is incredible.

In conclusion I want you the reader to take this in. Throughout the trials, storms, pain, and suffering my family endured. This is NOTHING in comparison to the anguish and suffering Jesus Christ endured on the cross. On the cross for OUR sins not his. Only then will we comprehend and appreciate God's love. He has given everything to us.

Through it all we have received victories in place of our trials. Joy instead of mourning because we put all our faith in the one who can do the impossible: Jesus Christ alone. My prayer is by reading my story you too will come to know him. No matter what you're going through in life, you are not alone. His loving arms are stretched out to you. Stretched out to all who seek his strength and love. I leave you with this passage from Matthew 11: 28-30.

"Come to me. All you who are weary and burdened, and I will give you rest. Take my yoke upon you and learn from me, for I am gentle and humble in heart. You will find rest for your souls, for my yolk is easy and my burden is light."

Amen.

"Know thy self, know thy enemy. A thousand battles, a thousand victories."

-SUN TZU-

Made in the USA
Columbia, SC
23 March 2019